EDMUND G. ROSS
# A Man
## of
# Courage

*Edmund G. Ross—senator from Kansas, governor of the Territory of New Mexico, with a deep commitment to freedom and justice for all.*

# EDMUND G. ROSS
# A Man of Courage

Arthur Elliot Harrington

PROVIDENCE HOUSE PUBLISHERS
Franklin, Tennessee

Printed in the United States of America

01   00   99   98   97            5   4   3   2   1

Library of Congress Catalog Card Number: 96–72450

ISBN: 1–881576–74–4

*Cover by Bozeman Design*

The author acknowledges the use of the following sources in compiling this volume—*The Life of Edmund G. Ross: The Man Whose Vote Saved A President,* by Edward Bumgardner, (Kansas City, Mo.: The Fielding-Turner Press), 1949; *History of the Impeachment of Andrew Johnson, President of the United States, by the House of Representatives and His Trial by the Senate for High Crimes and Misdemeanors in Office 1868,* by Edmund G. Ross, (Santa Fe, N.M.), 1896, and Memoirs of Edmund Gibson Ross, by Lilian Ross Leis. Unless otherwise noted, excerpts are from Bumgardner.

PROVIDENCE HOUSE PUBLISHERS
238 Seaboard Lane • Franklin, Tennessee  37067
800-321-5692

In memory of

Ethel Mary Ross Harrington
September 3, 1889–February 22, 1987
A granddaughter of Edmund Gibson Ross

# CONTENTS

# ACKNOWLEDGMENTS

I am deeply grateful for many cousins, descendants of Edmund Gibson Ross, who have helped in manifold ways in gathering information and encouraging the writing of EDMUND G. ROSS— A MAN OF COURAGE. Daughters of Clyde Ross, Ethel's brother, made Wyoming their home throughout most of their lives. They are our cousins Frances Ross Hoadley and Mae Fern Ross Hitchcock. They have added much to my motivation and research.

Cousins in Albuquerque have also added interest and information. Edmund Pitt (Ned) Ross and his wife Lila presented us a copy of Edward Bumgardner's biography *The Life of Edmund G. Ross.*

Many other cousins in Albuquerque have entertained us and encouraged us as we were doing research at the University of New Mexico.

I am deeply grateful for time given by Susan Cobb Beyer, granddaughter of Edmund G. Ross and daughter of Eddie Ross Cobb. Susan Beyer saved a very large collection of her grandfather's papers now still available at the University of New Mexico Library.

One of the most significant publications saved is a book first published in Santa Fe, New Mexico, in 1896 which is a full volume of 180 pages titled the *History of the Impeachment of Andrew Johnson, President of the United States.* The author is Edmund G. Ross. I am deeply indebted to the Santa Fe Archives for photocopying this for me. It has added greatly to one of the most significant portrayals of Edmund G. Ross. His vote saved the president from impeachment and saved the union of the states.

Lilian Ross Leis, the eldest daughter of Edmund G. and Fanny Ross, played a very significant role in writing her Memoirs of Edmund Gibson Ross. See appendix A for the memoirs which Lilian wrote for her family and descendants. I am grateful that Lilian knew Edward Bumgardner, also a resident of Lawrence, Kansas, and that she interested him in writing *The Life of Edmund G. Ross* and that she assisted him in the writing. This biography was published by Fielding-Turner Press in Kansas City.

EDMUND G. ROSS—A MAN OF COURAGE is a means of making the life of Edmund Ross more available to other descendants and interested student friends.

Cousin Hermagene Lacy found among her great-grandmother's papers a copy of Memoirs of Edmund Gibson Ross. I deeply appreciate Cousin Hermagene's interest and help. Her great-grandfather George Ross was the youngest to go to Kansas.

Mary Lynn McManus Toluchanian, a descendant of William Wallace Ross, Edmund's next-younger brother, compiled an extensive useful study which I have appreciated entitled, Ancestors and Descendants of Sylvester Flint Ross and Cynthia (Sinthy) Rice.

Many friends of Edmund Ross have made very significant contributions to this biography. Mrs. Gertrude Baccus, of Redlands, California, contributed a portion of the Ph.D. dissertation of her husband, the late Dr. Joseph Baccus, professor of speech at the University of Redlands and a fraternity brother. His title is *The Oratory of Andrew Johnson.*

Helen M. Hansen, curator of the Follett House Museum, Sandusky, Ohio, who, with assistance of a volunteer Patty Pascoe, found one hundred and four issues of the *Democratic Mirror*. They loaned these issues to me for a summer's reading.

The *Mirror* was published by Sylvester Ross Jr., Edmund's brother, and William S. Mills. Edmund worked for them in his teens as a typesetter, printer, and preserver of the newspaper.

Helen also presented a copy of her own publication *At Home in Early Sandusky* including pictures of early homes and the people who lived in them. This volume also includes the Oran Follett House which now houses the museum.

Rev. Al Eliason, First United Methodist Church of Milwaukee, introduced us to Frank P. Zeidler, a former mayor of the city. Zeidler referred us to Dr. Herbert W. Rice. Dr. Rice had recently retired from a scholarly career as professor of American history at Marquette University. He was deeply interested in Edmund G. Ross and the publication of the biography. Dr. Rice spent two full days at the Milwaukee Public Library selecting books from the shelves and noting items for copy. We are very grateful for Dr. Rice's help and friendship.

Sarah Thatcher McNeive is the receptionist at the Topeka Cemetery who guided us to the lot where Flint Ross, the four-year-old son of Edmund and Fanny was put to rest, March 7, 1862. Sarah McNeive also gave us good references to many people who were well-informed on the Ross family.

Vey Bassett Rutledge Spencer was an excellent guide to Dover and Wabaunsee Counties where many of the Ross family had lived during their early years in Kansas. Mission Creek and Ross Creek are just north of Dover. Vey lived near these creeks and was well-informed.

Mrs. Mildred Stoerker, a Pilgrim Place Neighbor and a native of Wabaunsee County, loaned us a book on the county. It shows that Edmund G. Ross and Edmund's father Sylvester accepted responsibilities on the county board in the year 1859.

The Kansas State Historical Society Museum in downtown Topeka holds many books and pictures related to the Ross family. A large portrait of Ross at the entrance shows the high respect they have for him.

Edward Bumgardner, of Lawrence, Kansas, included these lines of F. H. Hodder, late professor of history at the University of Kansas in June 1946:

> I am accustomed to think of Senator Ross's vote in the Johnson trial as the most heroic act in American history, incomparably more difficult than any deed of valor upon the field of battle.

I am most highly indebted to the University of New Mexico not only for the use of their libraries, but for the work of Karen Diane Shane, a graduate student who allowed me to glean information from her master of arts in history thesis. Most of her writing covers the years that Edmund Ross was governor of the territory.

I am deeply grateful for the work of Dr. Myra Ellen Jenkins, a most inspiring person and a well-informed historian of New Mexico. My wife Dorothy and I were visiting the archives in Santa Fe doing some research one day when we were introduced to Dr. Jenkins. We invited her to have dinner with us. After dinner we finished our visiting at her home where we were welcomed by her three friendly cats.

Dr. Jenkins came into the world too late to know Edmund G. Ross personally, but as a historian she was a real friend. She appreciated his role as a governor who was convinced that one of the greatest needs of the territory of New Mexico was public schools. Governor Ross spoke to the territorial legislature about the need for public education for all children and youth. We have waited too long to express our appreciation to Dr. Myra Ellen Jenkins personally. We join many friends, students, scholars, and those who worked in the archives in mourning her death. An interesting interview and information concerning her appraisal of Governor Ross can be seen and heard on videocassette. Dr. Jenkins's interview on KNME-TV at the University of New Mexico may be purchased by mail. Write: KNME-TV, 1130 University Blvd. N. E., University of New Mexico, Albuquerque, New Mexico 87102–1798. Ask for *Three Territorial Governors*.

I appreciate the great help of our grandson Donald E. Harrington for his super computer assistance. He's been recognized by the Claremont High School for his expertise and willingness to assist in their program.

I owe a great deal to my brother Dr. Edmund Ross Harrington, Ph.D. Ross is a retired superintendent of schools, Redondo Beach, California. He's experienced at publishing. He has helped me in the selection of writing style and has encouraged me to make this work a personal biography. Ross and Adelaide found a short autobiography while traveling in Kansas which appears in chapter 17.

William Harader, a public school teacher and a son-in-law, blessed us with proofreading. Our daughter Carol Harader has added her interest in my progress.

Dorothy and I enjoyed doing a lot of travel and research together. It was fun! I want to express here my appreciation for her patience while I was at the computer.

Others have expressed the desire to help in the distribution to the many cousins, descendants, and others who will have interest in EDMUND G. ROSS—A MAN OF COURAGE.

Cousin Frances Ross Hoadley has kindly accepted the invitation to proofread a prepublished copy of this story. She is an experienced proofreader, having had the experience of proofreading an autobiography of her husband and assisting with the publication. The title is *The Homestead Doctor* by Dr. Joe Hoadley, M.D. They can be reached at P. O. Box 386, Story, Wyoming 82842.

Cousin Edmund Pitt Ross (Ned) was also invited to read a prepublished copy of EDMUND G. ROSS—A MAN OF COURAGE. Other Albuquerque cousins were also invited to be members of the prereading team. Dorothy and I thank you all!

# Introduction:
# Ethel Ross and Her Family

EDMUND G. ROSS—A MAN OF COURAGE was inspired very largely by Ethel's devotion to her grandfather; she passed this on to her children. It is therefore significant that it be dedicated to her. She was born in Albuquerque, New Mexico. Her parents were Arthur and Mable Ross. Arthur was the first son of Edmund and Fanny Ross, born June 8, 1853, in Wisconsin.

Arthur married Mabel Lucy Griswold, June 24, 1886. The wedding was in Alameda, California. The newlyweds lived in the old Spanish Palace. There Arthur worked for his father, Governor Edmund G. Ross. They moved to Albuquerque in May 1889 at the end of Edmund's term as governor. Ethel was born just four months later in Albuquerque, September 3, 1889.

The family lived on their fruit ranch on the south side of Albuquerque. For seven years Edmund and Fanny Ross and Arthur and Mabel Ross and their daughter Ethel lived as close neighbors. These first seven years were very significant years in Ethel's life. She became devoted to her grandparents as well as her own parents. Thus Edmund Gibson Ross became a very important person to Ethel and remained so throughout her life. She passed this on to her family.

Ethel's father, Arthur Ross, brought his family to Ventura, California, where he died January 20, 1897. Ethel, then eight years old, and her two younger brothers Clyde and Rodney remained with their widowed mother Mabel Lucy Ross, a school teacher. They lived near their Griswold grandparents.

Ethel finished the grades with her mother as her teacher until the time of her mother's death. She then moved in with her Aunt Grace Griswold Weldon in Santa Barbara where she finished her four years of high school. She was then, for two years, a student at Pomona College, and in another year and a half, she earned a bachelor of arts degree at Stanford University. Ethel met Robert Elliot Harrington while working for him pitting apricots the summer of 1911. April 26, 1912, Ethel and Bob were married by a minister of the Congregational church. The wedding was held in the Weldon home in south Pasadena. They enjoyed a great honeymoon in a covered spring wagon pulled by a team of horses. They were the first campers in the Yosemite Valley that year. They brought home about twenty seedling pine trees in small empty milk tins. This was legal in 1912. They built their own home overlooking the Simi Valley. They landscaped their homesite with the trees, and the family grew up with the pine trees.

Bob and Ethel had four children—Arthur Elliot, Edmund Ross, Robert Weldon, and Beth Lorraine. We all grew up with the pine trees on a hill overlooking the Simi Valley and the ranches below. Dad was an apricot, walnut, citrus, and avocado grower and a dairyman.

I met Dorothy Louise Robinson at the University of Redlands. We dated, and soon Dorothy was a part of the family. We were married at her church, the First Baptist Church of Santa Ana, on September 25, 1937.

Our honeymoon was a trip to Boston in a new 1937 Ford Sixty Coupe, a wedding gift from her father and mother Archie and Elizabeth Robinson. We lived in Waltham, Massachusetts, with a great aunt named Susie Peabody, who needed a companion. It was in a lovely upstairs room of her New England cottage that I wrote my master's thesis entitled, "The idea of God in the Religious Realism of J. B. Prat." I was a student of Dr. Edgar S. Brightman at the Boston University Graduate School. I completed my theological training at Boston University School of Theology in the class of 1939. That June I received my elders orders and became a member of the Southern California Arizona Conference of the United Methodist Church.

In the summer of 1939 I was appointed as a minister on the staff of the First Church of Long Beach. We served Methodist churches in southern California for forty years, retiring in 1977.

On the following two pages are photographs of Ethel's family. The photograph below was taken in the living room in front of the fireplace when Beth was a babe in arms. Beth was born in March 1923. We older children already knew about our great-grandfather who, of course, was Edmund G. Ross.

*Bob, Dad Robert, Art, Mother Ethel, Beth, and Ross Harrington.*

*Mature family picture of Mother Ethel, Dad Robert, Beth, Bob, Ross, and Art at Mother and Dad's fiftieth wedding anniversary.*

# 1

## THE DAYS OF HIS YOUTH

Edmund was born December 7, 1826, in Ashland, Ohio. His parents were Sylvester Flint Ross and Cynthia Rice Ross who had been married in 1821. Sylvester was a descendant of James Ross, born in the year 1620 in Scotland.

Edmund was the third of fourteen children of Sylvester and Cynthia. They were deeply concerned about his health. Cynthia said that one of her tea cups would cover his tiny head. A Scotchman who lived across the street came over to watch the baby. He is reported to have said, "That boy will become a great man someday." This thrilled his mother deeply.

Edmund's father was both a farmer and a school teacher. Realizing that Edmund would not be strong enough to do farmwork, his father took him to Huron where Edmund's older brother Sylvester was an apprentice printer. Mr. Grey, owner of the *Huron Commercial Advertiser*, a weekly newspaper, gladly took Edmund on as an apprentice. Mr. and Mrs. Grey also welcomed him to their home where he and his brother lived for four years.

When Edmund was fourteen, Sylvester, his elder brother, bought Mr. Grey's press. They moved it to Sandusky, Ohio, and went into a partnership there with Mr. Mills. Edmund worked for them publishing the *Sandusky Mirror*.

The city was a very good nurturing environment for a growing young man in his teens. It was a county seat situated on Sandusky Bay, 105 miles from Cleveland and from Detroit. There was a good view of Lake Erie. The city was built on a large quarry of limestone, from which beautiful buildings and churches added to the city's attractiveness.

When Edmund was seventeen, a high school was built next to the Congregational church. He took singing lessons and was soon singing in a quartet which sang as a church choir. Fanny Lathrop, Fanny's sister and her boyfriend, and Edmund were the quartet. They sang on many occasions throughout the community. It was the beginning of a great courtship between Edmund and Fanny.

Sandusky was a part of the underground railway. Church people would take slaves into their homes providing them with food and a safe place to sleep. They would eventually arrive in Sandusky. From here someone with a small boat would take them across the lake to Canada and freedom.

As a young man, Edmund became involved in the abolitionist movement. The political divisions in the country and in Sandusky were considered by many to be religious issues.

The high school students had weekly writing assignments to express themselves concerning the issues of the day. These essays were then read before the student body. Edmund believed strongly in the sacredness of human life. He wrote a paper on the subject of capital punishment. This offended some of the faculty and administration so strongly that they threatened to expel him from school if he continued to write compositions of this nature. Edmund left the school taking his composition with him and had it published in the *Sandusky Mirror* where it was read by many more people than those in the high school.

When I was reading copies of the *Sandusky Mirror* loaned me by the Follett House Museum, I came upon this article on capital punishment and made a copy of it, portions of which appear in appendix B.

It has become obvious that Edmund Ross, in his early years, was already a man of courage. Edmund had completed three years of high school. He never went back to school for further formal education.

Edmund became an active abolitionist. There is no question as to where Edmund and many others in the life of the churches in Sandusky stood on such issues.

The quartet continued with their singing, and Edmund and Fanny continued their romance. Edmund was a young man of twenty years as of December 7, 1846.

# 2

# FAMILY LIFE

October 15, 1848, Edmund Ross and Fanny Lathrop were married. Although we were not there, Dorothy and I visited the county courthouse and verified the fact by taking a picture of the record. We were warmly greeted by the clerk who knew just where to find it. We also know that Edmund and Fanny celebrated their fiftieth wedding anniversary in Albuquerque, New Mexico, in 1898.

Edmund continued working with his brother Sylvester and partner Mills publishing the *Democratic Mirror*. Tragedy soon came to Sandusky as the year 1849 brought trouble to the Ross family and others. Asiatic cholera swept across the country. Sandusky was hit severely.

Elial J. Rice, the youngest brother of Edmund's mother, lived in Sullivan, Ohio. He knew about the epidemic and had not heard from his family in Sandusky. He drove there to see if he could help them. He returned home taking with him Edmund and Fanny and her sister. They remained in Sullivan until the epidemic was over.

The Ross family was not spared. Edmund's elder brother Sylvester was an early victim. His death is listed by Joel Roberts in the Cholera File of the Follett House Museum. Sylvester died July 25, 1849.

Rodney Lathrop, Fanny's father, died August 22, 1849. Rodney's daughter Emeline died the day before, August 21, 1849. (Bumgardner records another daughter also died during the cholera epidemic.)

Surviving the epidemic were Fanny's mother, who remained a widow with two sons, daughter Fanny, and son-in-law Edmund G. Ross. They lived together as a family.

Edmund and Fanny's daughter Lilian was born October 14, 1849. Edmund had returned to his work in the *Mirror* office, but it was not the same without his brother Sylvester there. Also the city was not the same. Edmund began thinking about relocating. Two years later the whole family, including Grandma Lathrop and her two sons, Fanny's brothers, moved.

## WHY LEAVE SANDUSKY?
## SANDUSKY WAS NOT THE SAME

The Asiatic cholera epidemic had changed many things in Sandusky. With Edmund's brother Sylvester gone, the *Democratic Mirror* was no longer the same.

Edmund had been working toward a career as a publisher for more than ten years. His training at Huron and Sandusky had given him many skills. He was now ready to move on; he was ready for advancement. The *Mirror* no longer offered him that opportunity.

Family life was different. Baby Lilian was now a two-year-old toddler. Fanny's mother was now a widow with her two boys. She was a good grandmother.

Edmund had become an abolitionist. He wanted to use his career to overcome slavery. He wanted to prevent the North and

# DEDICATION OF
# OHIO HISTORICAL MARKER
# SANDUSKY CITY CHOLERA CEMETERY

### SEPTEMBER 10, 1966

*Erected*
*In memory of*
*The pioneers of Sandusky, Ohio*
*Who gave their lives during the cholera epidemic*
*of 1849 to 1854 A. D.*
*During this great tragedy half of the 4000 population either fled*
*Or were called by death those remaining rendered worthy service*
*To their unselfish faithfulness we owe this tribute of reverence and love.*

— inscription on the monument

Text on obverse and reverse sides of Ohio Historical Marker —

## CHOLERA CEMETERY

Of the city's 5667 people in 1849, 3500 fled, and 400 of those remaining were victims of cholera. Most are buried here, some only in rough boxes in a common grave. The scourge came again in 1850 and 1852 but with less toll.

> "Dismay stalked abroad in the daytime
> and the drowsy night was hideous with
> the wailings of the disconsolate."

THE OHIO HISTORICAL SOCIETY

1965

## IN HONOR OF THE DOCTORS

Doctors, nurses and others assisted in fighting the cholera in 1849, aiding heroic citizens led by Foster M. Follett. Doctors Austin, Brainard, Lane and Tilden suffered illness and exhaustion, leaving Dr. Cochran alone among Sandusky doctors until aid came.

Drs. Ackley, Beaumont, Lauderdale and Spencer, and Messrs. Dolan and Miller of Cleveland; Drs. Banks, Caroland, Follen, Foote, Hughes, Lindsey, Ocheltree, Quinn and Raymond, and Messrs. Bailey, Hindale and Yorke, Mrs. Cowden and nurses from Cincinnati; Dr. Appleton of Philadelphia; Dr. Stanley of Canton; Drs. Evans and Peck of Akron; Drs. Glick and Teagarden of Mansfield; Dr. Vance of Urbana; and Mr. and Miss Rushton of Bellevue.

> "They came emphatically in our time of need, and
> faithfully and successfully did they minister relief to
> the distressed and the dying. Long will it be e'er the
> citizens of Sandusky forget their kindness."

ERIE COUNTY HISTORICAL SOCIETY

1965

Wording on marker by ........................... Charles E. Frohman
Arch donated by ..................... Grandchildren of John Lay, Sr.
Design of arch by ............... Frank W. Smith, Supervisor of Art
Sandusky Public Schools

the West from becoming slave states. Although the *Mirror* had been a voice in Sandusky, Edmund saw the real threat to freedom coming from the West.

Why go to Milwaukee? Edmund's father Sylvester and his mother Cynthia and their family were farming near Janesville. They were about fifty miles from Milwaukee and his next-younger brother William would be a good partner. They could possibly become publishers together. Milwaukee would be a good place to raise a family. Fanny was in agreement; she was ready to go. She would like to establish a home. She would like a place with good schools.

Fanny would enjoy having her mother Fanny Hayward Lathrop go with them. It became obvious that a large family like this would really need to go by ship. So the decision was made. They would pack everything in crates and the whole family would take the voyage together. It would be an exciting time.

# 3

## THE FIRST FAMILY VOYAGE WEST

What a great voyage! It was their first. The family included Edmund, Fanny, their two-year-old daughter Lilian, Grandmother Fanny Hayward Lathrop, and her two boys.

There had been much packing to do. Crates had to be put together and made secure. All clothing and personal effects were made available for the voyage, and they had to be kept separately for use upon their arrival.

Leaving Sandusky Harbor surely brought many memories to mind. I am sure that as they neared Put-in-Bay they recalled the happy times. The quartet had entertained many a party there. They would also recall many friends they were leaving behind.

There were also many anticipations. Fanny and Grandmother Lathrop and her two boys would be meeting Edmund's family for the first time. Arriving at the port near Milwaukee, they then traveled to the family farm near Janesville.

Their father, Sylvester Flint Ross, welcomed them home. Cynthia Rice Ross had prepared for their arrival. Was it to be a dinner or a barbeque? It included something good from the farm. They stayed at the family home for several days. It was not long before Edmund and his younger brother William were talking about employment.

Edmund and William found a good place for their family to live. They soon found jobs at the *Milwaukee Free Democrat* and enjoyed working there, as they agreed with its politics. The editor S. M. Booth was a cordial employer. His younger brother became a close friend of Edmund and William.

## LIFE IN MILWAUKEE

The first year they worked for Mr. Booth, 1854, was one of real challenge. Their publication discussed the issue of slavery. During the early spring, a fugitive slave named Joshua Glover was captured in Racine, Wisconsin, brought to Milwaukee, and imprisoned.

About a hundred sympathizers of Glover, joined by a larger number of Milwaukee citizens, demanded his release; it was refused. A group of men, including the Ross brothers, led by Booth, rushed toward the jail door swinging a large beam and breaking it down. A surrey rushed forward, and the men bundled Glover in a blanket and placed him in the back of it. The horses soon had them out of sight on their way to a waiting boat that took him across the lake to Canada and freedom.

Booth was arrested and tried in the United States District Court for violation of the fugitive slave law. He was convicted and sent to prison resulting in the suspension of the publication of the *Free Democrat*. The unemployed Ross brothers soon found better jobs with another Milwaukee paper, the *Daily Sentinel*, with Edmund as foreman and William as compositor.

The *Sentinel* is one of the largest papers in Milwaukee today. While doing research in Milwaukee, Dorothy and I drove around the buildings which now occupy a large part of the block.

Edmund and Fanny found a home large enough for the family and close enough for Edmund and William to go to work easily. Although the men liked their employment and the family were happy with their home, they watched for news concerning the Kansas Territory.

They knew that the stance Kansas would take would determine the stance of the entire country—slavery or no slavery. Edmund was married, had a family, and Fanny and her mother and their children were happily settled.

## STILL LOOKING TOWARD KANSAS

Two weddings took place in the Ross family in the spring of 1855. William married Mary Elizabeth Barry. His sister, Nancy Amelia Ross, married S. P. Wemple. After the weddings, the two couples took a trip to Kansas where they planned to settle and build new homes. George Ross, not yet sixteen years old, went with them and drove a herd of cattle for his father who intended to move the rest of his family as soon as the time was right.

Descendants of the Wemple family still lived in Topeka as of 1987. I had a brief telephone conversation with one of them. Illness prevented further visiting while we were doing research in Topeka.

The year 1856 was kind to Edmund. He was a young man in his early thirties, and was well-trained in his profession as a publisher. With a good salary as a foreman in the office of the *Milwaukee Daily Sentinel*, he and Fanny had a loving home and a family of three children. Grandma Lathrop and her two boys also lived in the home. As we know, Lilian was born in Sandusky. Their second child was Arthur, born June 8, 1853, in Milwaukee. Arthur is my grandfather. Pitt was also born in Milwaukee, November 15, 1855. Pitt is Ned Ross's grandfather.

Edmund and Fanny bought a new home after the newlyweds departed for Kansas. The new home was situated with a river view. It was very comfortable. We can be sure that grandmother Lathrop enjoyed this lovely home as she assisted with the care of the children.

Lilian tells about the fun they had as her father would take her on walks, and other occasions when he would be marching by their home with a group. See appendix A for more detail on these happy times. These involvements retarded plans for moving to Kansas, but it would come.

# 4

# ON TO KANSAS

With William and Mary Elizabeth Ross and Nancy Amelia and S. P. Wemple already in Kansas, Edmund had some direct communication with them. This spurred his interest to arrange to go as soon as it was practical. His father Sylvester and mother Cynthia and their family were also eager to go as soon as they could get equipped with covered wagons, oxen, flatbed wagons, horses, camping equipment, and sell or arrange for the care of their Janesville farm.

The news from William and Mary Elizabeth and Nancy Amelia and S. P. Wemple about life in Kansas and the need for more anti-slavery settlers to guarantee Kansas as a free state were additional motivations in their decision to prepare for the move.

> The flood of emigration desired by the opponents of slavery was already materializing. Edward D. Holton, a banker in Milwaukee, was the leader in the organization of a company of emigrants in that city. One of his first volunteers was the foreman in the [*Sentinel*] office. When

33

it became known that Mr. Ross was determined to go to
Kansas to fight for freedom, the printers of Milwaukee
called a meeting in his honor, April 5, 1856, and
presented him with a beautiful rifle made by a local
gunsmith. On account of his initiative he was soon recognized as the leader of the enterprise.

A group of friends gathered with them at their first camp and
gave them a farewell party. Target practice was the main festivity.
A sixty-year-old woman did so well that it was reported in the
Milwaukee newspapers. She was Mrs. Lathrop, Mrs. Fanny Ross's
mother.

Edmund's parents, Mr. and Mrs. Sylvester F. R. Ross, along
with their young daughter, drove their two-seated carriage ahead,
as Sylvester chose where the family would take cover. The
youngest two Ross sons, Charles and Walter, about fourteen and
ten years old, drove a covered farm wagon with a horse and a cow
tied behind it. Their route went to Dubuque and a banquet was
waiting for them.

The journey led up the Missouri River from St. Louis to the
mouth of the Kaw River. They then took a new road named the
Lane Trail in honor of Gen. James H. Lane who opened it. From
there they passed through Iowa City. There was no bridge for
crossing the Missouri so one of the wagons was drawn upon the
boat, which was then turned upstream, and pulled with a rope by
men on the bank. This process was repeated until the whole party
was on the other side of the river. This was quite a venture with six
large covered wagons each drawn by two yoked oxen.

"The Milwaukee emigrants arrived at Topeka at the most
exciting and discouraging time in the history of Kansas Territory"
(Bumgardner, 31). Freedom settlers found themselves often
confronted by those who were seeking to make Kansas a slave
state.

Early in 1856, William Ross, Edmund's brother, became the
partner of John Speer, owner of the *Kansas Tribune*. Later, in

December 1856, John Speer sold his share of the *Kansas Tribune* to
Edmund Ross. Edmund and William issued the paper for almost
two years.

> On August 26, 1857, the famous Grasshopper Falls
> Convention was held at which the free state men decided
> to participate in the territorial election to be held in
> October, instead of ignoring the territorial government
> by refusing the vote. Edmund Ross acted as secretary of
> that convention. In September, 1858, he retired from the
> [*Tribune*], and moved to Wabaunsee [County] where he
> was living the next summer when delegates were elected
> to the Wyandotte Constitutional Convention. He was
> elected to represent a district composed of four counties,
> was assistant secretary of this convention, and had a
> prominent part in shaping the constitution which was
> completed July 29, 1859, and under which, a year and
> half later, Kansas was admitted as a state.

On October 1, 1859, Edmund and William Ross organized a
new paper in Topeka called the *Kansas State Record*. It was here that
Edmund published some of his most important works.

# 5

## ORGANIZATION OF THE SANTA FE RAILROAD

Edmund Ross had a part in September 1860 organizing what later became the Santa Fe Railroad. The railroad was reorganized later when Ross was a member of the United States Senate, and he took part in the commencement ceremony.

Soon after this, Mr. Ross was called upon to perform another kind of public service. Until a short time before the railroad convention, there had been practically no rainfall in Kansas for more than a year. The year 1860 is known in Kansas history as the year of the great drought. Practically no crops were raised that summer, and the ensuing winter found thousands of poor settlers destitute of the necessities of life. A Kansas Relief Committee was formed, and contributions were received in the East and transported by the railroads without charge to the Missouri river. Relief supplies were distributed from Atchison to the different parts of the Territory. Mr. Ross had charge of the distribution in the interior. One of the

interesting souvenirs now in possession of the Kansas
State Historical Society is a bill of lading for a consign-
ment of supplies shipped to him at Topeka from
Atchison by *steamboat*. The abundant rains which
followed the great drought had again made the Kaw
navigable for small steamboats, even over the riffles at
Lawrence where a dam was constructed soon afterward.

*An early railway steam engine symbolic of those used by the Santa Fe. Courtesy—
Dorothy Wilgosz.*

# 6

# THE CIVIL WAR

I n August 1862, Edmund Ross sold the *Kansas State Record* to S. D. MacDonald and F. G. Adams (previously William left to represent the Pottawatomie Indians) and enlisted in the army following President Lincoln's plea for volunteers the previous month. Edmund became captain of Company E of the Eleventh Kansas Regiment which joined the regiment in Leavenworth commanded by Col. Samuel J. Crawford. Members of the company included George Ross, Edmund's brother, and N. P. Gregg, second lieutenant, John Kitts, James Conwell, and Henry Lindsey, all from the *State Record*. Lindsey, too young to enlist, was a drummer but became second lieutenant within a year. Ross had originally hired him on the condition that he stop swearing.

> Early in October the Eleventh Regiment was ordered south to assist in repelling a Confederate advance into Missouri and Kansas. It had several months of hard service under General Blunt, and took part in the Battle of Prairie Grove.

As they were marching through Cane Hill, Arkansas, on November 15th, the printers of Company E noticed the remains of a printing press lying in the street. The next day, "all quiet in camp," Captain Ross, Kitts and Major Plumb, who was also a printer, went back and examined the old printing equipment. There was a quantity of type, and they decided to gather it up, pick it out of "pi" and print an army paper. Kitts, who distributed the type, found it to be a tedious undertaking, as part of it was Cherokee type. It had been used to print a missionary paper called the [Cherokee Messenger].

An edition of 1200 copies was printed of the [Buck and Ball], the army paper which resulted. The name was suggested by the charge used for the muskets with which the men of the Eleventh were armed. They were long, heavy Prussian rifles that had been made in 1818, and were the only arms available at Fort Leavenworth when the regiment was called into service. They were loaded with three buck shot and a .72 calibre ball.

A copy of the [Buck and Ball] giving a description of the Battle of Prairie Grove is in possession of the Kansas State Historical Society. . . .

Early in 1863 the regiment was ordered to return to Kansas City. It was there reorganized as a cavalry regiment, and Ross became major by appointment of Governor Carney. The men were mounted, and their antique muskets were replaced by sabers and carbines. For nearly two years the regiment was employed chiefly in policing the territory along the Kansas-Missouri border—a much more disagreeable service than war against an open enemy, as the rebel guerrillas used every conceivable disguise and deceit while plundering and murdering Union sympathizers and detached parties of Federal soldiers.

In the spring of 1863 General Ewing directed Major
Ross to detail one or two companies of the Eleventh for
the protection of Lawrence, which, although situated
forty miles from the Missouri line, was all the time in
danger of guerrilla raids. At the bottom of General
Ewing's order, he wrote, "Could you go yourself?"
Interpreting this as part of the order, Major Ross took
his old Company E to Lawrence, and camped on a high
ridge just west of the town. While the company was in
camp there some of the residents of Lawrence were
annoyed by soldiers going to their wells for water and
by their loud singing and talking in the quiet of the
summer evenings. A petition to General Ewing resulted
in the removal of the company to a point in western
Missouri.

Within a few days after the removal of the company
there occurred the most inhuman performance of the
Civil War. On the morning of the 21st of August,
Quantrill appeared with some four hundred guerrillas,
massacred 180 unarmed citizens, and burned the greater
part of the noted free state town. Ross immediately
returned with his company, and this time camped on a
hill east of the stricken town. Here he remained on
guard for eight months. It was necessary for him to
maintain military control over the place in order to
protect the citizens and their property. His greatest
problem was in connection with the sale of liquor. Some
of his boys began to patronize the saloons that were
quite numerous in Lawrence, and to lose the self-control
necessary for dependable soldiers. Ross forbade the
saloon keepers to sell liquor to the soldiers, and when
the practice continued, he ordered the saloons to be
closed. This military order "interferred [sic] with business," and the liquor dealers protested and brought to
bear all the influence they could command. The Major
was obdurate, and when he learned that certain keepers

*Mrs. Edmund G. Ross (Fanny Lathrop Ross) and her family of maturing children awaited Edmund's letters during the war. Courtesy—the Kansas State Historical Society, Topeka.*

*Captain Edmund G. Ross in his Civil War uniform early in the Civil War. Courtesy—the Kansas State Historical Society, Topeka.*

were still selling, he took a detail of soldiers one Sunday morning, visited the places where orders had not been obeyed, had their kegs of liquor rolled out of the buildings, and literally made whiskey flow freely in the streets of Lawrence. He sometimes referred to this as a course of temperance lectures. A few days after this event, a number of Lawrence ladies called at his headquarters and presented him with their portraits mounted in a handsome photograph album which had this inscription on the first page:

> "Presented to Captain Ross
> by the
> Ladies of Lawrence
> For his manly defense of Temperance
> while in command of the Post."

In September, 1864, the Confederate General Price entered Missouri from Arkansas with a large army and hurried toward Fort Leavenworth intending to capture the army supplies there, and to lay waste to eastern Kansas. General Curtis, in command at the Fort, and General Blunt, with his "Army of the Border," with their limited forces could only hope to check Price until General Pleasanton could overtake him from the east. General Blunt made a stand a few miles east of Kansas City, and the Battle of the Little Blue was fought on October 21st. Part of the Eleventh Kansas, commanded by Major Ross, had been stationed at the crossing of the river with orders to detain the enemy as long as possible. The regiment had a day of severe fighting, and Major Ross had two horses shot from under him. Captain B. F. Simpson, who furnished Major Ross with another horse when his first one was killed, said: "All through that day he was one of the coolest and bravest." General Blunt was gradually forced back for two days, but on the third Pleasanton arrived and Price was compelled to retreat. The defeat of Price ended the last and most serious invasion of the North that was undertaken west of the Mississippi river during the war. The three days of fighting near Kansas City has been called "the Gettysburg of the West."

In the midst of all the above, Fanny and their family were not forgotten. Reassuring letters were mailed when the pressures of the battles lessened. Edmund's family was certainly part of the motivation along with his concern for all the people who had come with them from Milwaukee and others who preceded them. Following are copies of handwritten letters that he was able to send them from time to time.

We have already noted the times when Edmund's company camped within sight of Lawrence during the war. He surely found time to visit Fanny and his family by taking a brief break when the time was right. He did find such a time for a letter found by Adelaide Harrington at the Kansas Historical Society:

Fort Scott, Sept. 10, 1867

My dear wife,

I arrived here with the command at 1 o'clock today after a march of 130 miles through dust, rain, mud and am of course pretty well fagged out. We marched 20 miles yesterday through a terrible cold driving rain and such a depth of mud as I have never before seen anywhere in Kansas, and at night lay down and slept like beavers in our wet blankets on the wet muddy ground. However, we all got through in good shape and good spirits, every man ready to fight or foot race. I was officer of the day that night and had a good time poking around the dark and mud, posting pickets, and examining the guards.

Notwithstanding all the hardship of the march, we have now less sick than when we left Leavenworth, and the men are actually better able to stand another such march than when we started out.

Nathan and the boys arrived in camp this evening. I was very much gratified to hear that all were well and enjoying yourselves as much as could be expected. I hear today that the Rail Road stock matter has been arranged as I had directed, the stock all issued in your name so that you will have no trouble about it in case of any accident to me. I have not yet received that assignment that Brockway was to draw up and send me. I am feeling uneasy about it as we are ordered to leave here on Sunday next for Missouri.

There is fighting going on about 50 miles from here with success on our side so far. It may be all over before we get there, but both sides are concentrating heavy forces, so that there is a fair prospect of warm work before many days. We shall whip them of course, for Hell itself couldn't stand before such men as we have here.

Everything is going smoothly in the Company and I have reason to believe that the "boys" take a good deal of stock in their captain.

I have stood the march about as well as the strongest of them and think I shall be able to do about as good fighting as the bravest of them when it comes to that. At all events, my Topeka friends shall never hear it said of me that I have not performed my whole duty in the field, or exposed my men to any danger that I did not have to meet myself. I know I shall have your prayers that arrive and my children's name shall never be sullied by any act of cowardice of mine, let it cost what it will. Knowing this, I shall go into the fight doubly armed. If I fall, twill be a consolation to you, and a matter of pride to them to wear a name of which they will be proud as having contributed to something toward the success of this glorious cause. But we must not anticipate any such calamity, but look forward to the end of these troubles, when we can again muster our little flock in peaceful happiness. I am glad you are sending the children to school again, but don't neglect that home instruction of piety and truthfulness and pride in a good name which is so essential to make good men and women. It will be a relief to you during my absence.

When little Eddie begins to lisp, learn her first to speak my name and to know that she has a father who will be able with God's permission some day again fold her in his arms, never again to leave her. Learn our boys to reverence their father's name and example of self sacrifice that they may grow up, as I have done, to enjoy the blessings of a good and beneficent free government. Keep them out of the street and teach them to love their home, by making it always cheerful for them. Tell Lilie to wear my likeness, though I know it will not be necessary to do so to keep me in her memory—to study hard and be a good girl. . . .

Good night, my dear wife. Pray for me and learn the little ones to mingle my name with their nightly visions.

Your affectionate Hus.

# 7

# THE APPOINTMENT OF EDMUND ROSS AS SENATOR

Major Ross was discharged from military service on September 20, 1865. He had no plans to pursue a political career and went back to his newspaper work which was now in Lawrence where his family had been living while he was in the army.

Many candidates soon presented their claims for appointment to the vacancy caused by the death of Lane. [Senator Lane, a supporter of Johnson, experienced much opposition and committed suicide on July 1, 1866.] Colonel Crawford, who had become governor of the state, sent a note to Ross asking him to come to Topeka. On the 20th of July, 1866, an unusual thing happened in the Governor's office. A prominent candidate for appointment to the vacancy was a resident of Lawrence. Major Ross, supposing that the Governor wanted his opinion regarding the qualifications of that candidate, began to commend him. Governor Crawford interrupted him with: "We need a man with backbone in the Senate.

I saw what you did at Prairie Grove, and I want *you* for a senator." So, without solicitation on his part, and without previous intimation, Edmund Ross became a United States Senator.

Once again Edmund Gibson Ross with his quiet courage accepted an appointment he had not anticipated. Surely he would have preferred more time with Fanny and their children. Yet he knew it was a new and great responsibility to become a senator of the United States. It was an important time in the life of the country.

The preservation of the Union was the utmost goal of President Lincoln. It was likewise the goal of his successor President Andrew Johnson. The Republicans of the North believed the South should be punished. The new senator from Kansas was going to be facing these conflicts. He would take his stand with President Lincoln and with Vice President Andrew Johnson seeking reconciliation with the seven seceding states of the South. He would certainly also stand with Abraham Lincoln in recognizing the need of these states to have representation in the House and in the Senate.

## THE IMPEACHMENT AND TRIAL OF PRESIDENT ANDREW JOHNSON

Senator Ross in 1868 wrote a book entitled *History of the Impeachment of Andrew Johnson* which was first published in Santa Fe, where he was living in the former governor's palace. I was fortunate enough to secure a copy when we were doing research there at the archives of this capitol city, Santa Fe, New Mexico. In this history, Ross is standing with Mr. Lincoln who had, to a considerable extent, outlined his plan of reconstruction in his annual message to Congress. According to Ross, Lincoln spoke with a very humane, national, and patriotic purpose.

Edmund Ross, in chapter one titled "The Problem of Reconstruction," referring to Mr. Lincoln's plan, says:

The country had just emerged from a gigantic struggle of physical force of four years duration between the two great Northern and Southern sections. That struggle had been from its inception to its close, a continuing exhibition, on both sides, of stubborn devotion to a cause, and its annals had been crowned with illustrations of the grandest race and personal courage the history of the world records. Out of a population of thirty million people, four million men were under arms, from first to last, and sums of money quite beyond the limit of ordinary comprehension, were expended in its prosecution. There was bloodshed without stint. Both sides to the conflict fought for an idea—on the one side for so-called State Rights and local self-government—on the other for national autonomy as the surest guaranty of all rights—personal, local, and general.

The institution of negro slavery, the basis of the productive industries of the States of the South, which had from the organization of the Government been a source of friction between the slave-holding and non-slave-holding sections, and was in fact the underlying and potent cause of the war, went under in the strife and was by national edict forever prohibited.

The struggle being ended by the exhaustion of the insurgents, two conspicuous problems demanding immediate solution were developed: The status of the now ex-slaves, or freedmen—and the methods to be adopted for the rehabilitation of the revolted States, including the status of the revolted States themselves. The sword had declared that they had no constitutional power to withdraw from the Union, and the result demonstrated that they had not the physical power—and therefore that they were in the anomalous condition of States of though not States technically in the Union—and hence properly subject to the jurisdiction of the General Government, and bound by its judgment in any measures to be instituted by it for their future restoration to their former condition of co-equal States.

The now ex-slaves had been liberated, not with the consent of their former owners, but by the power of the conqueror as a war measure, who not unnaturally insisted upon the right to declare absolutely the future status of these persons without consultation with or in any way by the intervention of their late owners. The majority of the gentlemen in Congress representing the Northern States demanded the instant and complete enfranchisement of these persons, as the natural and logical sequence of their enfreedment. The people of the late slave States, as was to have been foreseen, and not without reason, objected—especially where, as was the case in many localities, the late slaves largely out-numbered the people of the white race: and it is apparent from subsequent developments that they had the sympathy of President Lincoln, at least so far as to refuse his sanction to the earlier action of Congress relative to restoration.

To add to the gravity of the situation and of the problem of reconstruction, the people of the States lately in rebel-lion were disfranchised in a mass, regardless of the fact that many of them refused to sanction the rebellion only so far as was necessary to their personal safety.

It was insisted by the dominant element of the party in control of Congress, that these States were dead as polit-ical entities, having committed political suicide, and their people without rights or the protection of law, as malcontents.

It is of record that Mr. Lincoln objected to this doctrine, and to all propositions that contemplated the treatment of the late rebellious States simply as conquered provinces and their people as having forfeited all rights under a common government, and under the laws of Nations entitled to no concessions, or even to consideration, in any proposed measures of restoration. That he had no sympathy with that theory is evidenced by the plan of restoration he attempted to establish in Louisiana.

It was at this point that differences arose between Mr. Lincoln and his party in Congress, which became more or less acute prior to his death and continued between Congress and Mr. Johnson on his attempt to carry out Mr. Lincoln's plans for restoration.

It is obvious that Edmund Ross, who wrote the quoted paragraphs above, was sensitive to the pain experienced by men and women and their families not only during the war but after the war was over. He carried the name of Maj. Edmund Gibson Ross during the latter part of that war. He suffered. He also knew that the men of the southern forces suffered.

The suffering was not over. The major issue now was to see that justice be achieved for all people whether they lived in the South or the North. As seen above, President Lincoln was seeking to bring reconciliation to all people, whether southern or northern, whether formerly slave or free.

Here we see Edmund G. Ross as a man of courage. We will be seeing more of that courage coming forth as we grieve the death of President Abraham Lincoln and the attempted impeachment of President Andrew Johnson.

# 8

# GETTING ACQUAINTED WITH ANDREW JOHNSON

The details as to how or when Senator Ross met the new president of the United States will probably never be known, but he undoubtedly came to know him long before the impeachment trial. It may be helpful for us to also get to know Johnson before dealing with the issues that were at stake.

Dr. Joseph Baccus, professor of speech at the University of Redlands, received his Ph.D. from the University of Wisconsin. He wrote his dissertation on the subject, "The Oratory of Andrew Johnson." He wrote:

> Andrew Johnson, without formal education, influential friends, wealth, or party organization rose to power largely because he became one of the greatest stump speakers America has produced. As President, he used the same methods in his celebrated swing around the circle, the effect on public opinion was unfortunate. His ability to alter his speaking methods, including his treatment of opponents, and to expand his mental horizons to include the national scene, account in large

measure for his difficulties as President. . . . His abilities as a speaker were utilized to give practical expression to his beliefs. He sought to better conditions for working classes of Tennessee by improving their educational advantages, reducing their taxes, fighting against high tariffs and other oppressive measures. Later, he became an advocate of the homestead law, an act which would give 160 acres of land to every responsible head of family. He spoke against extravagance, waste, and graft in the expenditure of the people's money. He opposed centralization of power in the federal government. . . .

It is my opinion that Edmund G. Ross would have shared many of these ideals. From his youth on, Ross was sensitive to people's needs as an abolitionist, a publisher, a major in the war, a friend of those who worked under his care, and a loving father.

## FOLLOWING LINCOLN'S POLICY—
## GETTING ACQUAINTED

At the death of Abraham Lincoln, Vice President Andrew Johnson became the president of the United States. Johnson sought to follow Lincoln's policy concerning the Union. He sought to keep the senators and the members of the House of Representatives of the southern states as legitimate members of the Senate and of the House. This he saw as being essential to the saving of the Union.

The Republicans from the North had a very different opinion. They believed that the people and the officially elected senators and representatives from the southern states should be punished.

President Andrew Johnson was considered by the Republicans an enemy because he was seeking to preserve the Union. Lincoln's policy was that the southern states should have representation which was considered necessary for the preservation of the Union, and Johnson supported that policy.

*Senator Edmund G. Ross.*

*The Living Lincoln, The Man, His Mind, His Times and the War He Fought*, edited by Paul M. Angle and Early Schenck Miers, is a tremendous source of Abraham Lincoln's writings which establish his position concerning the preservation of the Union. He was deeply committed to justice and the undergirding of the South.

The radical Republicans in Congress sought to keep the elected senators and congressmen from functioning in their office as duly elected. This created a split between President Lincoln and Congress.

This split continued to be a problem for President Andrew Johnson, who proclaimed that Congress was acting unconstitutionally. This conflict went on for more than two years.

## JUSTICE FOR ALL

Senator Ross had a great sense of justice, and, as a result, it is obvious that Edmund could not vote for the impeachment of President Andrew Johnson. However, Ross's decision was not due to personal friendship but because he was committed to doing what was right for Johnson personally and what was right and necessary to save the Union.

Justice was the real issue as far as Edmund Ross was concerned. It was a matter of saving the Union. If there was to be a Union, the people of the South should have all the privileges and power as the people of the North. The senators and the members of the House of Representatives elected by the people of the South should rightly be accepted in the Senate of the United States and in the House. Let us continue with Angle and Miers:

> According to Lincoln, there are persons in one section, or another who seek to destroy the Union at all events, and are glad of any pretext to do it, I will neither affirm or deny; but if there be such, I need address no word to them. To those, however, who really love the Union, may

I not speak? . . . We are not enemies, but friends. We must not be enemies. Though passion may have strained, it must not break our bonds of affection. The mystic chords of memory, stretching from every battlefield, and patriot grave, to every living chorus of the Union when again touched, as surely they will be, by the better angels of our nature. . . . The states have their status in the Union, and they have no other legal status. If they break from this, they can only do so against the law, and by revolution. The Union, and not themselves separately, procured their independence, and their liberty it has.

We are now ready to move into the final battle which ended in the impeachment trial. This trial was an attempt to get President Johnson out of office with what seems to be little thought given to the justice involved or to whether the new vice president would do as well as Johnson. So, now we turn to the events leading up to the Johnson impeachment.

# 9

# GETTING ELECTED AS FULL-TERM SENATOR

In Douglas County, S. A. Riggs, a lawyer from Lawrence, was a candidate for the state senate and a supporter of Ross as U.S. senator. John Speer, also a candidate, supported Solon O. Thacher for the U.S. Senate. At a primary election Riggs defeated Speer by one vote.

> There is a tradition that the election of the Riggs delegates resulted from a quarrel between two Douglas county farmers. A. F. Thomas and William Griffin lived on opposite sides of a country road. Both were Democrats. They became involved in a dispute over the ownership of a pig which divided its time between the feed lots of the Thomas and Griffin farms. So bitter did the quarrel grow that the two men became avowed enemies. Thomas even declared that he would change his politics and no longer affiliate with Griffin in local caucuses as he had done. On the day of the county election Thomas worked most of the day on his farm. Toward evening he rode to Lawrence on horseback and

arrived at the voting place just as the polls were about to close. He secured a ticket and was allowed to vote. The ballot which he cast caused the Riggs delegates to have a majority of one. So Riggs went to the legislature, and it was his adroit strategy in Ross's cause that secured the election of the Senator for the full term.

In the light of events that we shall see develop, the vote of Thomas in a local political contest is an injunction upon every citizen to exercise his right of franchise with intelligence and fidelity. It turned the scales in favor of Riggs, and had it not been for Riggs, Edmund Gibson Ross would not have been in a position to write his name in imperishable characters in the annals of America.

# 10

## THE IMPEACHMENT TRIAL OF PRESIDENT JOHNSON

Edmund Gibson Ross was at the age of forty-two when, as a senator in his second year, he faced the debate and rough political maneuvers of the impeachment trial of President Andrew Johnson. President John F. Kennedy in his volume *Profiles in Courage* recognized the stress that was involved in the trial. Readers may find the Kennedy chapter of special interest.

The Memoirs of Edmund Gibson Ross by Lilian Ross Leis, Edmund's daughter, and Edward Bumgardner's *The Life of Edmund G. Ross*, are also good resources. The official report of the proceedings of the Senate Court was published as a government document of 526 large pages of fine print containing more than a million words.

Andrew Johnson, a Southern Democrat, had been elected vice-president on the Union ticket with Lincoln in 1864. He was intensely Union, he had made a life study of the Constitution, and he was honest and courageous. When the appalling responsibilities of the presidency were suddenly thrust upon him, it was impossible for him, with a temperament entirely unlike that of Lincoln, to secure the co-operation of a Republican Congress even to the extent that Lincoln had done.

By refusing to sign a reconstruction bill containing provisions which he considered unconstitutional, Lincoln had incurred the wrath of the Radical Republicans, violently expressed in the Wade-Davis Manifesto. The antagonism of Congress toward President Johnson was a continuation of that already developed toward President Lincoln. Johnson, with the same desire that Lincoln had possessed to have the Southern states resume their places in the Union with as little delay and controversy as possible, was confronted by a bitterly partisan Congress that was determined to permit no such amicable treatment of the subdued South as that contemplated by the Executive Department.

Secretary Stanton, under the direction of President Lincoln, had prepared a tentative plan for reconstruction which had been submitted to the Cabinet and unanimously approved. When the Secretary of War abandoned this plan, adopted the tyrannical attitude of the Northern politicians, and sought to become a military dictator over conquered provinces, his usefulness to the Johnson administration was at an end. The President naturally asked for his resignation. When he refused to resign, the President suspended him and placed General Grant in the War Department. General Grant served as Secretary of War from August, 1867, until Congress convened in December.

The Senate then refusing to sanction the suspension of Stanton, he resumed his position as Secretary of War. The situation became intolerable to the President. His determination to preserve the dignity of the Executive branch of the Government brought down upon his head a storm

*Vote on impeachment of President Andrew Johnson in the Senate May 16, 1868. Courtesy—the Kansas State Historical Society, Topeka.*

of opposition unparalleled in partisanship and vindictiveness. It is difficult for another generation to conceive the bitterness of passion that was then manifested.

The Tenure of Office Bill, intended to prevent the President from removing appointive officers, was passed and sent to the White House. At a cabinet meeting all the members, including Stanton, declared the bill unconstitutional and advised the President to veto it. This he did. It was passed over his veto, but his legal advisors told him, and he believed that Congress had no constitutional power to compel him to keep in his cabinet a man who had been appointed by a former president.

On February 21, 1868, the President issued an order of removal against Secretary Stanton and reported it to Congress. This action, apparently in violation of the

Tenure of Office act, seemed to offer a pretext for impeachment proceedings. The House of February 25th reported to the Senate articles of impeachment against the President and demanded his trial and removal from office. The Senate was organized as a Court under the constitutional provision, the ordinary business of the Government was neglected, and the nation was on the verge of chaos for three months.

Senator Ross was one of the few men in Congress who [maintained control]. He was a Republican. Party loyalty was regarded by many as more important than personal convictions. He had been through all the bitterness of the slavery fight in Kansas, and for three years he had stood against exasperating guerrilla warfare. He was not in sympathy with the President, personally or politically. Notwithstanding all this, when the senators took an oath to do impartial justice to the President in his trial, Mr. Ross meant what he said in that oath. He determined to lay aside all prejudice and be true to his oath.

As the trial of the President progressed it became more apparent that it was an effort to depose an executive simply because his policies of administration did not agree with the ideas of a majority of the members of Congress. To speak plainly, the radical members of Congress did not intend for the President to be given a fair trial. In the words of Mr. Evarts, one of Johnson's counsel, he was to be "sacrificed upon an altar erected to the savage demon of party hate and party rage." Let us notice a few of the expedients that were employed in a scheme to convict regardless of recognized principles of fair play:

The participation of Senator Wade in the trial as a judge of the President was a palpable violation of propriety and justice. As President *pro tem* of the Senate, Mr. Wade would have become president if Johnson had been deposed. Over the protest of Senator Hendricks, who cited the constitutional provision prohibiting the vice-president from presiding at a trial of the president, Wade assumed authority as a member of the Court of Impeachment. His attitude was an assumption of prejudgment and egotism. Not only was he to become president, but he and his fellow conspirators had the audacity to select in advance a cabinet for him as the successor of Johnson. Butler, the leader of the prosecution, was to be secretary of state; and General Grant was promised the nomination to succeed Wade in the presidency if he would promise to retain Wade's cabinet! Every act that Senator Wade performed during the impeachment proceedings was in self-interest and in brazen contempt of justice.

It is an accepted rule in court procedure that the presiding judge shall rule on the competency and admissibility of evidence. Contrary to the established custom, the Senate made a specific rule taking this prerogative from Chief Justice Chase who presided at the impeachment trial. Assuming this authority, the Senate exercised it in an arbitrary and partisan manner, repeatedly rejecting proffered testimony in the President's favor. The majority of the members of the Senate voted for the conviction of the President after refusing in seventeen instances to hear testimony offered in his behalf.

General Sherman as a witness was not permitted to testify that as ranking officer of the Army he had advised the President that the good of the service required a new secretary of war.

With Secretary Wells on the stand, the defense desired to show that the Cabinet had advised the President to veto the Tenure of Office bill as unconstitutional. The other members of the Cabinet would also have testified to this. The Chief Justice ruled the testimony admissable. By a vote of the Senate the decision of the Chief Justice was overruled. Neither was Mr. Wells permitted to testify that the Cabinet advised the President that his power to remove officers appointed by President Lincoln was not restricted by the Tenure of Office act.

At a Cabinet meeting it had been agreed that a test case as to the constitutionality of the law should be presented for determination in the courts. Evidence regarding this was offered by the defense, and was rejected.

It is worthy of mention here that all the members of the Cabinet, with the exception of Stanton, remained firm in their loyalty to the President. It was suggested to Secretary Seward by a committee from the prosecution that if he would withdraw his support from Johnson, he would be allowed to continue as Secretary of State under the new regime that would be set up after the conviction. His indignant reply was: "I'll see you damned first. The impeachment of the President is the impeachment of his Cabinet!" In fact, the veto message on the Tenure of Office act had been prepared by Seward.

The Senate was composed of fifty-four members: forty-two Republicans and twelve Democrats. Thirty-six votes would be necessary to convict the President. All Republican . . . senators were expected by the managers of the impeachment, and by their party leaders throughout the country, to vote for conviction, and it was taken for granted that the Democratic senators would vote for acquittal. The verdict was to be determined by partisan prejudice, and not upon law and facts.

Although the radical enemies of the President were assuming that he would be convicted, a few Republican senators were maintaining a silence during the trial that was irritating to the prosecutors, if not ominous for their plans. For the purpose of placing these gentlemen on record, a "conference of senators" was called for May 11th. This was merely a partisan caucus of the Republican senators to ascertain whether the prosecution was likely to succeed. At this session six Republican senators: Fessenden, of Maine; Fowler, of Tennessee; Grimes, of Iowa; Henderson, of Missouri; Trumbull, of Illinois; and Van Winkle, of West Virginia, declared that the evidence so far introduced was not sufficient to convict the President as charged. There was still a possibility that the prosecution would succeed without the votes of these six senators. Even if all of them and all of the twelve Democrats should vote for acquittal, and all the remaining Republicans should vote for conviction, the vote would be thirty-six to eighteen, and the President would be ousted. There was one Republican, however, who would not announce his verdict in a preliminary poll. Senator Ross, of Kansas, would not decide until he had heard and weighed all the evidence, and in consequence he refused to go on record.

It was obvious that in order to convict the president, one vote was needed from either Senator Ross or one of the other six Republican senators.

# 11

## CASTING THE DECIDING VOTE

The six men who had declared themselves opposed to the impeachment of President Johnson received a deluge of threatening mail. Edmund Ross had not declared himself, yet his mail was as heavy and critical as the others, if not more so.

> . . . Tampering with the jurors in an ordinary lawsuit is never tolerated; in this, the most important case ever tried in America, the jurors were subjected day and night to personal appeals, while they were bombarded with letters and telegrams containing petitions, advice, demands, threats and offers of bribes. The "Union Congressional Committee" sent this telegram to the different states:

> Washington, D.C., May 12, 1868.

> Great danger to the peace of the country and the Republican cause if impeachment fails. Send to your senators public opinion by resolutions, letters and delegations.

> Robert C. Schenck, Chairman.

Senator Ross, having had but little experience in political turmoil, was more sensitive to criticism than the six dissenting senators; yet his constituents were the most radical, and he was subjected to the most insidious propaganda. His brother, William Ross, who was in Washington at the time, received a letter offering him $20,000 if he would only reveal how the senator would vote.

The probable outcome of the trial was being discussed in the room of General Butler, one of the managers of the prosecution. A senator remarked that no promise could be secured from Ross as to how he would vote, when Butler exclaimed: "There is a bushel of money; how much does the damned scoundrel want?"

Some of the gallant prosecutors called at the studio of Vinnie Ream where she was working on her Lincoln statue, and terrified her with the absurd demand that she secure Ross's vote for conviction or suffer the consequences.

On the day before the vote was to be taken, this telegram was received from Leavenworth:

Senators Pomeroy and Ross:

Kansas has heard the evidence and demands the conviction of the President.
D. R. Anthony and 1000 Others.

It now seemed probable to Senator Ross that his would be the deciding vote. The consequences would be momentous. What he was about to do might precipitate or avert a change in our form of government. It might bring a revolution; but whatever the outcome, it was most important to him that the accused President should receive justice. He felt the responsibility, and prayed for wisdom and strength that would enable him to do his duty.

On the Friday night preceding the eventful 16th of May he could secure but little rest. Spies, advisers and pleaders followed him all night. In the evening he went to the residence of Senator Pomeroy to get a copy of the Anthony telegram which had been delivered there. He was invited to remain for supper, and was thus compelled to listen to Senator Pomeroy's arguments in favor of conviction. At half past eleven he was in a restaurant conferring with two senators while a friend was waiting to interview him. The strain upon his nerves had become almost unbearable. A reporter who saw him an hour after midnight said that his gait and countenance showed the personification of mental anguish. When he finally reached his lodgings he was sought by General Sickles who remained till four o'clock determined to save him for the prosecution.

When morning came he went, under the surveillance that had become constant, to the home of his friend Perry Fuller in the hope of securing a little privacy. He took breakfast there, and wrote a telegram in answer to the one from Anthony:

"I do not recognize your right to demand that I vote either for or against conviction. I have taken an oath to do impartial justice according to the Constitution and laws, and trust that I shall have the courage to vote according to the dictates of my judgment and for the highest good of the country."

E. G. Ross.
To D. R. Anthony and Others.

As the time approached for the historic session of the Senate Court, Senator Ross made his way to the Capitol. In the Senate lobby he was met by his colleague from Kansas with a warning that a vote for acquittal would mean political death for him, and a threat that it would also be investigated on a charge of bribery.

*Courtesy—the Kansas State Historical Society, Topeka.*

At twelve o'clock, noon, the Chief Justice took the chair, and the Sergeant-at-Arms made the usual proclamation opening the Court. With the exception of Senator Grimes, all the senators were present. There had been an adjournment of four days to allow for the recovery of Senator Howard, of Michigan, who had been unable to attend on Tuesday. Today he was in his seat to the great satisfaction of the prosecution. Two days before, however, Senator Grimes had suffered a paralytic stroke, and the managers of the prosecution were really in hopes that he would not appear to vote for acquittal. Senator Williams, of Oregon, moved and it was carried that the Chief Justice in directing the Secretary to read the several articles of impeachment, should direct him to read the eleventh article first. The vote was to be taken upon each article by the Chief Justice demanding the verdict from each senator, the names to be called in alphabetical order.

Senator Fessenden rose to move that the voting be post-poned for half an hour, when Grimes, almost helpless, was carried into the Chamber and lifted into his seat. The court was now full, and the voting would proceed.

It was a solemn and dramatic scene. Two inner rows of desks in the semi-circle around the Chief Justice were taken by the senators; the outer rows of desks and chairs filling the rear of the Chamber were occupied by members of the House. The managers of the prosecution were placed at the left of the Chief Justice, and the counsel for the defense at his right, and the galleries were packed with people who had been admitted by printed tickets. For the first time during the trial, the gravity of the occasion seemed to settle over the Chamber. An intensity of feeling was evident, and the silence was oppressive. As the Chief Justice rose to call the vote of the first senator, he grasped the desk before him as if his emotion would prevent him standing without support.

Slowly the votes were cast, all as predicted in the poll that had included all but the senator from Kansas. The first break in the monotony of the roll call came when Senator Fowler, in reply to the interrogation of the Chief Justice, answered in such a low tone that most of the audience heard only the second of the two words he spoke. A flutter of triumph was felt by the enemies of the President, and a throb of despair by his friends until the presiding officer called upon the senator to repeat his answer. Then his "Not guilty" rang out so unmistakably as to cause an audible reaction. . . .

The suspense was most intense when the venerable Chief Justice demanded:

"Mr. Senator Ross, how say you, is the respondent, Andrew Johnson, President of the United States, guilty or not guilty of a high misdemeanor as charged in this article?" Senator Ross replied, "Not guilty!" The supreme act of his life had been performed.

At the conclusion of the roll call the Chief Justice announced:

"Upon this article thirty-five senators vote 'Guilty,' and nineteen senators vote 'Not guilty.' Two thirds not having pronounced guilty, the President is, therefore, acquitted upon this article."

The seven recusant senators had all stood by their ideas of justice. An immediate vote on the other articles would have been as unsatisfactory and perhaps more emphatic. Instead of proceeding to vote on them, the managers of impeachment proposed and secured an adjournment until May 26th. This was plainly in the hope that some of the Republican dissenters could be whipped into line. It meant ten days more of uncertainty, and, for Senator Ross, ten days more of insult and threats, even of abduction and of assassination. The first word he received from Kansas after the vote was another telegram from D. R. Anthony:

Leavenworth, Kansas, May 16, 1868.

Hon. E. G. Ross, United States Senator,
Washington D.C.

Your vote is dictated by Tom Ewing, not by your oath. Your motives are Indian contracts and greenbacks. Kansas repudiates you as she does all perjurers and skunks.

D. R. Anthony and Others.

On the same day another telegram came from Kansas. This one from Topeka:

Unfortunately the rope with which Judas hung himself is mislaid, but the pistol with which Jim Lane killed himself is at your service.

L. D. Bailey.

Many editorials in Kansas newspapers were no less vicious. For instance, the [*Oskaloosa Independent*] said:

On Saturday last Edmund G. Ross, United States Senator from Kansas, sold himself, and betrayed his constituents; stultified his own record, basely lied to his friends, shamefully violated his solemn pledge . . . and to the utmost of his poor ability signed the death warrant of his country's liberty. This act was done deliberately, because the traitor, like Benedict Arnold, loved money better than he did principle, friends, honor and his country, all combined. Poor, pitiful, shriveled wretch, with a soul so small that a little pelf would outweigh all things else that dignify or ennoble manhood.

Mr. Ross was chairman of the Senate Committee whose duty it was to transmit to the President bills that required his consideration. During the progress of the trial the routine of legislation had been at a standstill. When the Court adjourned on that Saturday afternoon the Senator had several bills in his possession which required immediate attention, as the time for their consideration would expire on Monday. With these bills in hand he took a street car to deliver them to the President. James G. Blaine, then a member of the House, was on the same car. As Ross got off the car near the White House, Blaine said, "There goes the rascal to get his pay." It was a source of much satisfaction to Ross when Blaine long afterward wrote in his "Twenty Years in Congress": "In the exaggerated denunciation caused by the anger and chagrin of the moment, great injustice was done to statesmen of spotless character."

. . . On the 26th the Court reassembled to pass on the ten remaining articles of impeachment. Votes were taken upon two articles, and the result was the same as the vote taken on the 16th. There being no prospect of conviction on any one of the remaining articles, the Court of Impeachment adjourned sine die. The historian of the future was relieved of the necessity of recording that in 1868 the Executive branch of our Government became subordinate to the Legislative, but the seven devoted senators were to pay the price. No one of them was ever elected to office again. The fight of many years was necessary before the prophecy of Senator Ross in his fist letter home came true. On May 22nd, he wrote on a sheet of Senate stationary:

> Don't be discouraged, dear wife, it's all coming out all right. This storm of passion will soon pass away, and the people, the whole people, will thank and bless me for having saved the country by my single vote from the greatest peril through which it has ever passed, though none but God can ever know the struggle it has cost me. Millions of men are cursing me today, but they will bless me tomorrow. But few knew of the precipice upon which we all stood on Saturday morning last.
>
> Your aff Hus.

I debated the wisdom of including some of the above terrible accusations, but they are a part of the story. We can better appreciate Edmund's strength after knowing these accusations. I can better appreciate his strength after knowing what he heard yet still having the courage and faith to believe that he was right, fair, and just. In our current perspective we can see that he not only saved President Johnson from impeachment but saved the union of the then-existing states of our United States of America.

# 12

## HOME AGAIN TO KANSAS

Senator Ross kept his position in the Senate until the end of his term on March 4, 1871, having served nearly five years as the senator from Kansas. After returning to Kansas, Edmund Ross found that time had begun to heal the wounds. The people there were not as belligerent but were more unconcerned and aloof, causing Ross and his family to feel excluded socially.

Ross went back to his earlier vocation by starting a paper in Coffeyville, Kansas, at the end of 1871. He enjoyed becoming a publisher once again. It provided opportunities to address people on current issues.

In February 1872, he spoke to the people of Kansas opposing another term of office for President Grant. A couple months later, April 10, he became a delegate to a liberal Republican convention in Topeka.

Soon after, on April 23, a tornado hit Coffeyville and completely destroyed the plant. He was inside the printing shop when it hit. It tossed him around, but, fortunately, he was unhurt.

*Edmund and Fanny Ross's children (left to right): Arthur Ross, Eddie Ross Cobb, Kay Ross, Pitt Ross, and Lilian Ross Leis.*

Edmund returned home to be with his family at Lawrence where they had lived since prewar days. He was associated with newspaper work there, part of that time as the publisher of the *Standard*. In 1876 Edmund was the presidential elector in favor of Tilden.

Four years later in February he bought the *Standard* and the *Leavenworth Press* consolidating the two papers. That fall he became the Democratic candidate for the governor of Kansas opposed by the incumbent who won.

He wrote a series of articles entitled "Historic Moments" appearing in *Scribner's Magazine*. In an article he described how he felt at the time he rose to cast his vote as a senator. He wrote:

> The Chief Justice, with apparent emotion, propounded the query, "How say you, Senator Ross, is the respondent, Andrew Johnson, guilty or not guilty under the article?"

> At this point the intensity with which the gaze of the audience was fixed upon the figure then on the floor was beyond description or comparison. Hope and fear seemed blended in every face, instantaneously alternating, some

with revengeful hate predominating as in the mind's eye they saw their dreams of success, of place, and triumph dashed to the earth; others lighted with hope that the President would be relieved of the charges against him, and things remain as they were. Not only were the occupants of the galleries bending forward in intense and breathless silence and anxiety to catch the verdict, but the Senators in their seats leaned over their desks, many with hand to ear, that not a syllable or intonation in the utterance of the verdict should be lost.

Conscious that I was at that moment the focus of all eyes, and conscious also of the far-reaching effect, especially upon myself, of the vote I was about to give, it is something more than a simile to say that I almost literally looked down into my open grave. Friends, position, fortune, everything that makes life desirable to an ambitious man, were about to be swept away by the breath of my mouth, perhaps forever. Realizing the tremendous responsibility which an untoward combination of conditions seemed to have put upon me, it is not strange that my answer was carried waveringly over the air and failed to reach the limits of the audience, or that a repetition was called for by distant senators on the opposite side of the chamber. Then the verdict came—"Not guilty"—in a voice that could not be misunderstood.

The die was cast. The best, or the worst, was known. The historic trial of the age was practically ended. American institutions had successfully endured a strain that would have wrecked any other form of government. The resumption of low conversations, of the fluttering of fans, and scraping of feet, mingled with guarded expressions of satisfaction or disappointment, according to the predilection of the speaker, all the little confusions of a crowded audience, were resumed, until order and silence were somewhat forcefully enjoined by the presiding Chief Justice.

# 13

## INVITATION TO NEW MEXICO

Edmund Ross received an invitation late in the year of 1882 to go to New Mexico. It included free transportation to attend a fair at Albuquerque. The fair was being held to promote the development of the territory.

He accepted the invitation hoping his deteriorating health would get better while on the trip. Edmund enjoyed this new place, his health improved, and in the end, he decided to stay there and carry on his newspaper work. After the fair he was invited to make a trip to the mountains and wrote a series of articles on the natural resources of the territory.

Edmund sent for his family late in July of 1884 and they settled in Albuquerque. That fall he joined in the presidential campaign for Cleveland.

> In April, 1885, he went to Washington and called on President Cleveland to present recommendations for appointment as governor of New Mexico. The President was very gracious to him and promptly issued a

commission for the position he had solicited. Returning to the West, Mr. Ross stopped at Lawrence, his former home, where his daughter [Lilian] was living. Here he had a pleasant visit. The old prejudice against him on account of his famous vote was laid aside and he was given a warm reception. There was a parade led by the Lawrence band, a public meeting at the opera house, and everything was done to assure him of a genuine welcome.

The next day he continued his journey toward Santa Fe where he was inaugurated as governor. He insisted upon a more simple ceremony than the prevailing Spanish custom would have demanded. When this was over he went to Albuquerque where, on July 22, 1885, a banquet was given in his honor at the Aztec Club.

# 14

# THE GOVERNOR OF THE
# TERRITORY OF NEW MEXICO

Governor Ross served four years as the governor of the territory. The first year, his appointment by Cleveland was not yet verified by Congress and was very strenuous. He moved to Santa Fe, where he stayed at the Palace Hotel while the Old Spanish Palace was being prepared for him. These quarters were not only inconvenient but prevented Ross from having good office space for performing his duties as governor. Due to his opposition to alcohol, as governor, he did not allow wine to be served at the Old Palace, even on New Year's Day. Fanny and several of their now-adult children had the opportunity to enjoy family life together again. They also served as staff members.

The family became aware of many conflicting elements within the territory. The large variety of people often made it difficult to keep peace in the land. From early years people had migrated from Spain, Mexico, and areas to the South. The governor was confronted with violence in the territory. There was a great need for land and resources development, resolution of conflicts over grazing lands and ownership of inherited land, solutions for difficult political and cultural conflicts, and the development of public schools.

Aside from a variety of cultures, there was also a variety of occupations which oftentimes created conflicts. In the early years, sheepherding was the dominant agricultural occupation. The sheep were pastured in the grassy fields and mountain sides. However, after the Civil War, farmers from the eastern states migrated westward bringing with them their cattle. The cattlemen sought to pasture their beef on the same hillsides and in the same valley pasturelands. This created conflict over the use of water as well as the natural grass of the area.

There were also political conflicts. At least one time these conflicts led to violence. It was election time. At one of the rural polls this conflict between the Republicans and the Democrats was so intense that when it became known that one side was winning, a representative of the other side shot into the polling place to deter them from turning in the ballot. Another pollster shot out the light ending the violence.

It is significant that the University of New Mexico, beginning during the Ross term as governor, should, one century later, inspire a student, Karen Diane Shane, to write a master's degree thesis in

*Palace of the Governors, Santa Fe, New Mexico.*

*Fanny Lathrop Ross, the first lady of New Mexico, and Edmund G. Ross while governor of the Territory of New Mexico.*

history on the subject of Edmund G. Ross as governor of New Mexico. Karen introduced her thesis with the following paragraph:

> Appointed by a reform President Cleveland, Governor Edmund G. Ross was charged with cleaning up the politics in New Mexico and was often involved in acrimonious political infighting. He began his term by tackling The Santa Fe Ring dominating the politics in New Mexico.

Territorial issues included statehood, violence, economic development, and most notably, Spanish and Mexican land grants. Ross, ever mindful of his reputation, simultaneously fought to undermine the ring's influence and to bring New Mexico into the mainstream of national politics. This was not an easy balancing act in the late-nineteenth century.

The historical background of New Mexico did not help the governor accomplish many things he thought important in preparing the territory for statehood. Following are examples of the historical factors involved.

Colonization took place in 1540. Francisco Vasquez de Doronado opened up the Spanish borderland, but his failure to find anything economically exploitable deterred development in the far north. Colonization occurred along the Rio Grande, and Spaniards, Indians, and missionaries experienced a difficult existence.

Spain's hold endured for nearly three centuries. The area remained isolated and economically stifled. Skilled artisans and homebuilders were scarce on the northern frontier. The only port of entry from Europe was through Mexico.

Late in the fall, after harvest, caravans made the long trek from Santa Fe to Chihuahua. They drove thousands of sheep and carried animal skins, Indian blankets, pinion nuts, brandy and wine, and Indian captives to be sold as slaves.

## THE UNIVERSITY OF NEW MEXICO

The University of New Mexico began while Edmund G. Ross was still governor of the territory of New Mexico. He struggled to lay the foundations for public education. He desired to establish an American school system before New Mexico was admitted as a state.

Dr. Myra Ellen Jenkins was the chief of the historical services division and state historian, State Records Center and Archives, Santa Fe. Yet in her historical research she came to have a deep appreciation for the stand that Governor Ross had taken.

Dr. Jenkins presented an article entitled "Early Education in New Mexico" which was published in the *National Education Association School Review*. In that article she wrote:

> New Mexicans can justly boast of the fact that their land has a longer continuous history than any other part of the United States. But the story of how they provided for their young for nearly three hundred years before the passage of the first real publication act in 1891 is not one which they can tell with due pride.

Jenkins went on to say:

> The teachers' association had a powerful ally in the
> blunt incorruptible Governor Edmund G. Ross who on
> the first day of their meeting delivered his message to
> the legislature.

This message was one of the best defenses of public education on record:

> It therefore becomes a pre-requisite in this of
> all Countries, that intelligent education shall
> characterize all walks of life, and to see that
> this is properly inculcated in the youth of the
> State, is the highest duty and most sacred
> function of government. Ignorance is slavery.
> Intelligent education is freedom. No commu-
> nity can prosper, and no nation can long
> preserve its liberty, that fails to provide for
> the education of its youth. No man can be
> properly equipped for the intelligent
> discharge of the duties of citizenship without
> a reasonable thorough common school
> education. A State owes itself for its own
> protection, as well as to its youth, to provide.

*Myra Ellen Jenkins, chief of the Historical Services Division and state historian, State Records Center and Archives.*

The governor continued working for public education throughout his four-year term. However, the national administration had changed, and one month later Ross was replaced. His successor L. Bradford Prince, fortunately, was likewise committed to a system of free, public education for the Territory of New Mexico.

A good summary of Edmund G. Ross's term as governor follows:

> He was Governor of New Mexico for four years, guiding
> the Territory in its development toward statehood,
> and protecting with all his power the interests of the
> actual settlers against scheming land-grabbers who were

attempting to secure private control of New Mexico's vast
natural resources. Although it was against strong Spanish
influences, he was outspokenly in favor of establishing a
genuine American school system before the admission of
New Mexico as a state. So vigorous and successful was he
as Governor, that he became known as "Old Montezuma."

There were several friends and family members of Governor
Ross who saved his publications, addresses, letters, and records of
the four years he was governor. Chief among these was the late
Susan Cobb Beyer. Susan was the daughter of Eddie Ross Cobb.
Eddie Ross was the younger daughter of Edmund G. Ross. We
visited Susan Beyer at her home in the autumn 1986, and we came
to have a deep appreciation of the work she had done in collecting
letters and papers of her grandfather. These Edmund G. Ross
papers are now available on microfilm in the Coronado Room of
the library of the University of New Mexico.

Historically, Edmund Ross had been surrounded by a host of
friends who look back upon his four years as governor with deep
appreciation. These include not only his descendants but
numerous scholars, archivists, educators, and political successors.

*Edmund Ross Harrington, Adelaide Stevens Harrington, and Susan Ross Cobb Beyer.*
*Farewell after rich visit with Susan.*

# 15

## TWENTY CREATIVE YEARS IN NEW MEXICO

Governor Ross resigned when Harrison succeeded Cleveland as the president of the United States. He resumed his former profession and worked for awhile on the *New Mexican*, a paper that was published by Max Frost, who was an old political opponent. In 1896, while still working with the paper, he wrote a 180-page book called the *History of the Impeachment of Andrew Johnson, President of the United States*. Some of this information has been included in chapter 11.

Edmund Ross wrote two historical articles for the *Forum* in 1895. "A Previous Era of Madness and its Lessons," published in July, discussed the anger of the northern leaders after the Civil War and its results. The second article, "Political Leaders of the Reconstruction Period," published in October, dealt with members of the Senate and the House during his time as a senator. "In accordance with his own character, his reminiscences of these men were courteous and gracious, although his memories of relations with some of them could not have been pleasant" (Bumgardner, 99).

Edmund Ross also served during one administration as secretary of the State Bureau of Immigration. He went to Deming where

*Edmund and Fanny Ross at the time when he was publishing the* Deming Headlight. *Tablecloth on left has in print* "DEMING."

for three years, he published the *Deming Headlight*. He then went back to Albuquerque and opened a job printing office. He lived in his orchard home throughout the last years of his life. His elder son Arthur and his wife Mabel and their three children were neighbors.

These were good years for Edmund and Fanny. It was a time when they could be with their grandchildren. Though Ethel, Clyde, and Rodney would have still been quite young, I can imagine that while Grandpa and Grandma were living in a neighboring house on their fruit ranch they found time to play some games together or perhaps go for a buggy ride together. These were good years on the fruit farm, but they did not last as long as the family would have liked.

*Edmund and Fanny's two daughters are Lilian Ross (right), the elder of the two, and Eddie Ross Cobb, who with her husband was a well-known photographer in Albuquerque. Lilian was the eldest member of the family. She also wrote the memoirs of her father which are in appendix A. Courtesy—the Kansas State Historical Society, Topeka.*

The family gathered together in New Mexico to celebrate Edmund and Fanny's fiftieth wedding anniversary in 1898. Fanny's earthly life was completed November 12, 1899. They had enjoyed a happy life together for fifty-one years after rearing a family of six children (having lost one while in Topeka).

Edmund had a high respect for women. He believed in equal rights for women. His relationship with Fanny, I believe, had much to do with his own self-esteem. It also had much to do with respect for all people.

Their Christian faith and their life in the church had a great deal to do with his high regard for all persons. This high regard, at times, must have been difficult when dealing with persons who had little regard for the value of others.

*Edmund G. Ross with three grandchildren—his namesakes (left to right): Edmund Ross, of Albuquerque; baby, Edmund Fessenden Cobb, of Albuquerque; and Edmund Ross Leis, of Lawrence, Kansas.*

Need it be said, Edmund greatly missed Fanny after her passing. It was a time of loneliness. His elder son Arthur and Mabel and their three children had moved to Ventura to live near Mabel's family. Edmund's eldest daughter and her husband and family had stayed in Lawrence, Kansas. Although the other members of Edmund's family remained in Albuquerque, he was lonely in his orchard home.

Edmund's eldest living son Pitt was very thoughtful of his father and may have made a home for him during part of his lonely years. Eddie, Edmund's youngest daughter, still lived in Albuquerque, as did his youngest son Kay who may have lived near him on the fruit farm for part of the eight years after Fanny's death.

In one of the last letters Edmund had written to Fanny from Washington, he had closed with this statement: ". . . Millions of men are cursing me today, but they will bless me tomorrow" (Bumgardner, 89). Edmund's prophecy in many ways was fulfilled in these last years as many friends of earlier years came to visit him with words of praise and gratitude.

# 16

## LATTER YEARS OF VINDICATION

**M**any visitors brought joy to Edmund Ross in his latter years. He was able to pursue the activities he most enjoyed. He was a publisher at heart, and he continued with his homestead, the fruit ranch, and the printing shop.

His daughter Lilian traveled from Lawrence, Kansas, to be there on his eightieth birthday, December 7, 1906. She undoubtedly traveled by rail on the tracks that her father had built and dedicated.

This was a high occasion for the family and particularly for Edmund. Those present for the celebration were Lilian, Pitt, Eddie, and Kay. His daughter Fanny, who married George Miles in 1897, lived in California. Arthur, who had moved his family to Ventura, California, died January 20, 1897. To have four of his surviving five children gather together to celebrate his eightieth birthday brought him great joy.

Other friends visited Edmund during these later years. None of them brought him more joy than "the Kansas Hermit." Gen. Hugh Cameron was a friend of Edmund Ross who was so sickened at how Edmund had been treated after President Johnson's impeachment trial that he withdrew from society until those who mistreated

*General Cameron, Edmund Ross, and friends taking a buggy ride in Albuquerque. Courtesy—the Historic Photo File of Walter Haussamen.*

the senator admitted their wrongdoing. Thus, Cameron removed himself from society and became known as "the Kansas Hermit."

Cameron lived on a bluff above the Kaw River a few miles from Lawrence for many years. He lived among the branches of a large tree. He allowed his hair to grow down to his waist. He was a unique man attracting attention when he made shopping visits to Lawrence. During 1906, he collected letters expressing the change of public opinion from what was thought directly after the 1868 impeachment trial. Some of these follow.

> Quotations from a few of these letters will indicate the general tenor of them all. Col. R. T. Van Horn, who was a member of the House of Representatives at the time of the impeachment trial, wrote:
>
> Gen. Hugh Cameron:
>
> I was in Washington at the time and while not in agreement with Mr. Ross, yet we were never other than

friends, and for one I have never questioned the conscientious purity of his motives and actions. I was at home when the House voted impeachment, and I have long since congratulated myself that this accident omits me from the record.

Please, when you meet Mr. Ross, convey to him my respect, confidence and, in the logic of history, my congratulations on the place his name now occupies as one of the rare examples in history where honors, position and applause have been set aside for the approval of one's own sense of right duty.

As the years roll by the patriotism and self-sacrifice of that vote will be more than vindicated, as posterity [sees] the calamities that it avoided.

R. T. Van Horn.

Captain Alfred C. Pierce, who commanded one of the companies of the Thirteenth Kansas Regiment, testified as follows:

He was an honest and devoted man to principle. He was brave in the performance of duty. . . . His vote was cried down at the time by a lot of stay-at-home rangers. I have been conversant with the politics of Kansas for fifty years and have been acquainted with most of her public men. Senator Ross was one of the greatest and bravest of them all.

Wiliam H. Carruth, a beloved professor in the University of Kansas and author of "Each in His Own Tongue," wrote:

It has not been said often enough that in the best judgment of the present day, Senator Ross voted wisely, and that an incalculable calamity would have befallen the nation had he not cast the vote for which his fellow citizens execrated and even threatened him.

It goes hard with us to admit that he was wiser than the majority of us. . . . Major Ross returned to his state, faced obloquy and slander, and earned the living of a

poor and honest man, with the same silent endurance
with which he met the stress of the great impeachment
trial. . . .

When General Cameron came to Albuquerque and gave these
letters of regard for Edmund Ross we can imagine what Edmund
might have thought or said: "Now let me depart in peace; for I
have seen truth and justice prevail" (Bumgardner, 109). At one
point, he did say, "I will be a bigger man dead than I have been
alive" (Bumgardner, 109–10).

> On May 8, 1907, less than two months after he had
> received these evidences of good will from his old
> acquaintances in Kansas, an attack of pneumonia termi-
> nated the career of Edmund Gibson Ross. The news of
> his death caused the publication of statements secured
> by General Cameron, and called forth many editorials
> and eulogies all over the country, all expressing the
> universal verdict that he was an honest, wise, patriotic
> and self-sacrificing man.

His memorial service was conducted by the pastor of the
Presbyterian church at Albuquerque. It was attended by the
governor of New Mexico and his staff from Santa Fe. Adjacent to
the grave of his dear wife Fanny Lathrop Ross, Edmund Gibson
Ross was given the honors of the Grand Army of the Republic by
Carleton Post, of which he was a member.

> At a spot in New Mexico from which at twilight the
> beautiful afterglow over the mountains can be seen
> reflected from the shining waters of the Rio Grande rest
> the mortal remains of the patriot who, in the United
> States Senate Chamber, on the 16th of May, 1868, cast the
> momentous and far-reaching vote in American history.

# 17

# EDMUND G. ROSS TELLS HIS OWN STORY

My brother Edmund Ross Harrington and his wife Adelaide Stevens Harrington visited the Kansas Historical Society of Historical Records during a trip April 20–28, 1993. Among other interesting items they came upon a handwritten autobiography which Adelaide graciously typed. This is Edmund Ross's story in his own words.

> Born at the town of Ashland, then Lorain County, Ohio, Dec. 7, 1826—was apprenticed to the newspaper business at Huron, Ohio, in September 1837, in the office of the *Huron Commercial Advertiser*, a weekly newspaper published by Henry C. Gray.
>
> In 1841 removed to Sandusky City, Ohio, and completed my apprenticeship.
>
> During the next few years traveled over considerable portions of Ohio, Indiana, Illinois, Wisconsin and Michigan, as what was then known as a "tramping"

journeyman printer—after which returned to Sandusky City and settled down.

In October 1848, was married to Miss Fanny M. Lathrop, at Sandusky City, and in 1852 returned to Milwaukee, Wis., remaining there until 1856, engaged as a job printer in the office of the *Milwaukee Free Democrat* and the *Milwaukee Sentinel.*

In May 1856, removed to Kansas, conducting a colony of Free State immigrants with their families, from Milwaukee, traveling around through Wisconsin, Iowa and Nebraska, by oxteams and immigrant wagons, to the then disputed country, the new Territory of Kansas—the control of which was then in contention between the free-slavery element of the South and the anti-slavery element in the North. Locating at the young city of Topeka, the then prospective capital of the proposed new State of Kansas—and at once took the field with the Free State forces to repel armed invasion by the pro-slavery forces.

At the close of that campaign, which practically settled the question of slavery in that territory, engaged in the publication of the *Topeka Tribune* with my brother W. W. Ross, thus taking an active part in the discussion and settlement of the then paramount question of slavery in Kansas—first in the field of arms, carrying a musket in what was then known as the Free State Army of Kansas, and for some years after, till the admission of Kansas as a State, engaged in moulding the general formative conditions of the prospective state being a member of the Convention held at Wyandotte in the summer of 1859 which framed the Constitution under which Kansas was finally admitted to statehood, and on the adjournment of that Convention began the publication of the *Kansas State Record* at Topeka in the interest of the adoption of the new Constitution by the people and its acceptance by Congress.

In the summer of 1862, after the admission of Kansas to the Union and the settlement of all questions attending the formation of the new State, I enlisted in the Army of the United States as a private soldier and engaged in raising the Eleventh Regiment of Kansas Volunteers for the war of the Rebellion, to serve for "three years during the war."

At the organization of that Regiment was elected Captain for the Company I had raised and at once took the field with Gen. Thomas Ewing as Colonel, and served till the close of the war, the last year as Major of the Regiment— something over three years—the field of operations covering those portions of Missouri and Arkansas lying between the Kansas and the Arkansas Rivers.

During my service, this Regiment took part in some fifteen engagements.

Upon the close of the war in 1865, I went back to the newspaper business as editor of the *Kansas Tribune*, publishing at Lawrence, Kansas, and on the 25th of July 1886, on the death of Senator Lane, was appointed by Col. S. J. Crawford, then governor of Kansas, to succeed Senator Lane in the U.S. Senate, and was elected by the Kansas Legislature of the succeeding winter—of that term, to March 4, 1871.

The record of membership of the U.S. Senate was practically devoid of public interest except in the matter of the impeachment and trial of President Andrew Johnson. Elected as a representative of the radical element of the Republican party, it was expected that, as a matter of course, by my partisans, that I would support the

*Edmund G. Ross in his retirement days in Albuquerque. Photo was taken at the home of Pitt Ross, his son, circa 1906–1907. The home was located in south Albuquerque near the present intersection of Pacific and Barelas Streets. Courtesy—the Historic Photo File of Walter Haussamen.*

impeachment afterwards brought against President Johnson. As was then well-known, I was not a supporter of his policies of administration and it was supposed that I would support the movement for his impeachment and removal but upon careful analyzation of the charges brought against him, I failed to discover any valid ground for his removal and though realizing at the close of the argument that the decision of the case rested upon my own vote, and that to vote against his conviction would result in my removal from the Senate at the expiration of my term, I chose the certainty of expulsion rather than become an instrument in what I came to believe during the investigation would be an act amounting to a public crime in the interest of a partisan faction which was seeking control of the Government for the accomplishment of partisan ends.

At the expiration of my term in the Senate, I returned to Kansas to find all avenues of employment in the newspaper business closed against me on account of that vote, and after some months of idleness began the publication of a weekly newspaper at Coffeyville down on the southern border of Kansas. A destructive cyclone (even the elements of the air seemed to "have it in" for me) struck me and scattered my building and printing office and material for miles over the prairies—utterly destroying presses, and everything that was destructible—landing me, stunned and bruised, on the ground a considerable distance from where my building had stood—and my last dollar gone.

From that I went again to journey work—and some seventeen years ago my wanderings brought me to New Mexico, where for a time I found occasional employment.

On the installation of President Cleveland, in 1885, I was appointed governor of this territory, and after four years and the election of General Harrison to the presidency, I was again, and very promptly, relegated to private life and the printer's case—and am now by turns, printer, farmer, gentleman at leisure, author, philosopher, tramp—but never a SOREHEAD.

—Edmund G. Ross

# APPENDICES

## A. Memoirs of Edmund Gibson Ross
## by Lilian Ross Leis

Edmund Gibson Ross, the subject of the story, was born on the seventh day of December in the year 1826 in the little town of Ashland; Ashland County, Ohio, was where his father was teaching school. Edmund was the third child, the second son.

The elder son Sylvester, bore his father's name, Sylvester Flint; the sister was Sylvia, and the younger boy was given the name of an uncle, brother of his grandmother (Anna Gibson) and her grandfather whose name was Edmund Barton.

It is curious to note how the family names continue down the line of younger generations. A little story related to his mother in later years may not be without interest. It was during the Civil War and I was visiting at the farm where only one son remained at home, a boy of sixteen, who could not leave his father alone. I've often thought of my grandmother's fortitude, with three sons in the volunteer army and one in the militia, but one was also called into active service. We were speaking of my father's early life, of his delicate health, the serious attack of scarlet fever which was feared would end his young life.

Sitting by the fireplace, with its huge backlog, grandmother, in an old-fashioned rocker, her hands on the arms, her fair face encircled as with a halo by the frill of her white lace cap, all aglow with the memories awakened by these early years. As I watched her earnest blue eyes, from my corner on the large old sofa by the chimney—I recalled the picture vividly. She had bought a new blue and white tea-set just three weeks before my father was born, and he was so small that one of the tea cups would cover his face. She continued with reminiscences—"An old Scotchman who lived across the street from us took a great interest in the baby and would sit by him by the hour. One day he had been watching him a long time, while the baby was asleep. As he rose to go, spreading his hands above the child, he exclaimed, 'The "bye" will be a great "mon" one day, mark my words. The "bye" will be a great "mon" one day.' Why, his words fairly thrilled me," she added.

Although delicate from the first years of his life, the boy continued to live and grow, combating, with great care from the family, the usual foes of childhood. Owing to his lack of health that a boy should possess, he was taken by his father to a printing office in Huron where the older brother had preceded him, and placed him under the charge of Mr. Henry C. Grey, owner, editor, of the *Huron Commercial Advertiser*, a weekly newspaper.

His home, during this period of apprenticeship, was in the family of Mr. Grey, in company with his brother Sylvester. For Mrs. Grey he formed an affection which continued through life. They even continued with correspondence in later years during the Civil War.

In 1841, Sylvester Ross purchased the printing plant and removed it to Sandusky, where he formed a partnership with Mr. Mills, the firm name being "Mills and Ross," and the title of the newspaper being the *Sandusky Mirror*. In politics, it was democratic.

In this business, Edmund G. Ross remained eight years, at first, working nights and mornings in the office, and attending school, becoming a general favorite with his associates.

Of his political tendencies he says, quoting from an old notebook, "In 1844, though not then of voting age, took sides somewhat actively for a minor with the anti-slavery movement, in what then was then known as the 'Liberty Party,' and afterward with the organization known as the 'Free Soil Democratic Party,' organized at Buffalo in 1848, and cast my first vote at Sandusky, Ohio, for Martin Van Buren, New York, the candidate of the party for the presidency, with Charles Francis Adams of Massachusetts for vice president.

"In 1846 I attended the public high school working at the case in the *Democratic Mirror* printing office mornings and evenings to 'pay my way.' The custom at the school was to devote one afternoon per week to the reading of compositions by pupils. On one of these occasions, tiring of the uniform practice of a large number of pupils devoting themselves to reading prevailing extreme religious ideas then prevailing, I produced a 'composition' representing opposite views which I held. A number of so-called orthodox clergy men were present, as were also the school directors. These gentlemen at once and vigorously objected to the tenor of my way, and I was informed that I must cease, at once, the production of such essays or leave the school. I chose the latter course, protesting that if I could not have the same privileges permitted the other students, my self-respect prompted me to leave at once. That was the last of my school attendance, or of efforts to the attainment of a scholastic education."

He failed to continue the account of this episode and I [Lilian] will endeavor to do so from "scraps" of conversation I heard one time at my grandmother's. A sister, Anna, whom I assume was at the same school at the same time, heard an amusing account which was expressed by some of the pupils.

Grandmother said, turning to my mother, "Were you one of the girls that cried, Fanny?"

The principal gesture he made was to return to the office, and print copies of his paper—or dodgers, as I think they were sometimes termed—distribute them, and even tack them up in places where they would be read. To have allowed him to read his paper expressing his convictions, would have given it much less publicity.

Mr. Lathrop, a leading Universalist of the city, a direct descendant of the pioneer Congregational minister of 1634, and also a highly respected citizen, had two daughters, both singers. With a friend of the elder sister and Ross, the four formed a quartet for their pleasure and constituted the church choir. The younger sister was a schoolmate. This must have been, and doubtless was, the most carefree period of his life with work, school, and the social element, "singing school," picnics, and trips to Put-in-Bay. The evenings with music from incoming steamers on the lake formed pleasant pictures and evidently held a deep place in their memories.

Edmund's father purchased a farm in Wisconsin, near Janesville; and thither the young man, his health never robust, sadly in need of recuperation, journeyed, principally on foot, accepting lifts from farmers, sometimes a stagecoach, stopping for rest at towns where he "subbed" for printers who also desired a rest. He traveled in this manner through Ohio, Indiana, and Illinois, and spent the summer on the farm.

In going through Chicago, he put up at the Trees House. In later years he continued to make that his hotel whenever in the city.

After the months spent with younger brothers and sisters, and with health and strength renewed, he was, in his own words, and with a twinkle in his eye—"In too great a hurry to get back, and this time availed himself of the more 'rapid transit,' the stagecoach."

On October 15, 1848, he was married to Fanny M. Lathrop, daughter of Rodney and Fanny Hayward Lathrop.

In 1849 an epidemic of Asiatic cholera swept over the country and wreaked great havoc in the city of Sandusky. Sylvester Ross was a victim. He was a brilliant young man with apparently a fine career in the future. His wife and young son were left behind. I knew a lady who said he was the handsomest man she ever saw, tall and dark, much like his father, Sylvester.

Just at this period there came to the distressed family a young uncle of the brothers', their mother's youngest brother, driving his own conveyance from Sullivan, Ohio. Not being able to learn of the relatives—good or ill tidings—he determined to brave the dangers of the infected city, from which all who could, were fleeing—and to bring away whomsoever he could, and he did. Returning to his home, he took Edmund, his wife, and sister Anna, who later became Mrs. Judge Bennett of Silver City, New Mexico. They remained away until their return was considered advisable, but in the meantime, Mr. Lathrop, and his eldest daughter Esther, then Mrs. John Walter, and the youngest Emmaline, of sixteen years, had succumbed to the scourge within the same week. Mrs. Walter and her father had been heroic in their efforts to aid others and paid the penalty.

The return of the travelers found Mrs. Lathrop with a desolate house and two young grandsons to care for; their father, Mr. Walter, having left home in the spring on a long journey.

Except for the courage of the uncle this story would probably never have been written, for it was, without a doubt, his heroic efforts that the others remained to "carry on."

This young man was Elial J. Rice, who was then studying for the ministry. He was a graduate of Hamilton College, New York, and superintendent of schools in Evansville, Indiana. Rice was the first professor elected to the first faculty of Kansas University, president of Baker University, Baldwin City, Kansas. He died in Trinidad, Colorado, where he had gone in search of health, April 7, 1873. He was beloved by the congregation of which he was pastor and respected by his townsmen.

About six months after the return to Sandusky, Mr. Ross made another journey to the home in Wisconsin. After a short visit in Janesville near the farm, he secured a position on the *Milwaukee Free Democrat*, his brother William Wallace, two years his junior, joined them there. My Grandmother Lathrop, having no further home cares, came to us and I remember how I, a three year old, used to enjoy going up to her room, sitting on a low couch in front of her wood fire, and watching her swiftly moving knitting needles. She wore white lace caps set back on her head revealing her dark wavy hair. She seemed always trim and neat and very small. She was the daughter of a Revolutionary soldier, Samuel Hayward, and a pioneer in Casinovia, New York, where she was born and married.

Our home the first winter was on Spring Street Hill, a long walk, I think, from the office. I remember the boys, as my mother called them, wearing long cloaks, not coats, with plaid linings. In the spring they moved nearer the business, and in June a brother was born—Arthur—and also Barnum's Circus pitched a large tent on a vacant corner nearby. My father took me one evening, especially that I might see Tom Thumb, the carriage given him by Queen Victoria, and the polar bear. He was always thoughtful about taking his children and instructing them, wherever and whenever he could do so. This could have been a very desirable location, for by winter, we were transferred to a very pleasant block and near the surrounds. Across the street on the left corner was a "female" academy, where my father's sister Nancy attended school, and she lived with us. On our own side of the street, at left was a very pretty home where I often played, and at the corner to the right a Presbyterian church. All the residences were attractive. And here occurred another incident which I will relate.

One day, at the noon meal, I noticed much talking and excitement and the hurrying away. A young man named Booth, a friend of Uncle William, had come home with him. He was a brother of the editor of the *Democrat*. After the three had returned to the office, as I was sitting in my small rocker, my mother said to me, "If you will

take your doll and sit on the porch, you may see your father go by."
At once I did so, taking my seat to the top of a long flight of steps,
or so it seemed to me to be then, since the home stood high above
the street. After what seemed a long time, there came a rumbling
sound, growing louder, until there appeared a long column of men,
two abreast and marching "double quick." My special interest was
in watching their feet—that made the strongest impression on my
mind, and then I saw my father and his brother side by side, and he
looked up and smiled while running. This was known as the
"Glover Rescue." A runaway slave had reached Milwaukee in
safety, only to be taken and thrust into jail by officers awaiting the
owner or emissary to return the slave to his former bondage. All
this I learned later and more clearly from a friend, who, at the age
of seventy-five, visited in my home—Mr. John A. Rastall, a former
Kansas editor, and who was one of the boys in the crowd at the jail.
The men in the "mob," for such it was, demanded the prisoner or
the keys. Being refused, they secured a long pole, and as many as
could grasped it, swung it to and fro, until with sufficient force it
crashed in the door of the jail. A wagon was commandeered and
the Negro rushed in to it, when someone in the crowd called out
"He has no hat—give him a hat," about fifty hats and caps were
thrown into the wagon. The Negro was sent away over the lake to
Canada in safety, eluding the officers who arrived too late.

Prominent in the crowd, riding a white horse, and a leader of the
movement, was S. M. Booth, owner and editor of the *Free
Democrat*. And, in consequence of this occurrence, he lost his
property and eventually left Milwaukee, becoming one of the
editors of the *Chicago Tribune*, a position he retained until the time
of his death, a few years later.

The second year, the Ross brothers entered the employ of the
*Milwaukee Sentinel*. E. G. was foreman and manager of the job
office, a position he retained until leaving for Kansas in 1856.

My father's solicitude for his family during these early years
recurs frequently to me. Concerts and even an opera to which I
was taken were an extra care, but never considered an annoyance
to him. On long Sunday afternoons, I sat with my mother beside
a window, with their songbooks, and he with his tuning fork. The
prettiest books were brought to me—"Little Ferns" and
Anderson's Tales, "Auntie Wonderful" stories, and others, and

always pretty bindings. I had not such a wide collection to choose from as have the children of the present day, but I had all that could be found. He was truly a home-loving man.

In 1885 William Wallace married a little French girl, whose parents had been political refugees from France. Her father died in London, and her mother, presumably with friends or relatives, had drifted to Milwaukee, and then left her only child an orphan. She was very pretty with large dark eyes. I was taken to see them married and they returned with us to our home, as William lived with us. But the stay with us was of short duration. William Ross had become imbued with the spirit then urging men to rally to the cause of the Negro, and to make the territory of Kansas a Free State. After a visit at the home farm, and when spring came, in company with a sister and new brother-in-law, he departed for the New West. A curious wedding trip, but the two brides were full of courage and enthusiasm, and the future seemed full of hope. My father took his family to the farm to say farewell and witness the departure.

The party for Kansas consisted of William and his bride, his sister Nancy Amelia and her husband S. P. Wemple, along with a brother in his early teens. George Ross who accompanied them, drove a herd for his father in advance. For the elder Ross had determined to follow his sons later.

The following year was our last one in Milwaukee though not decided upon then. We had a pleasant cozy home, a nine-room cottage, painted almond with green and latticed porticoes and porch. The windows from the living room looked down over the river, and we could watch the steamboats pass under the swinging bridge and railroad trains come and go. This was quite near the lake and high above the street. My greatest pleasure was a walk to the lake. And often times we would all go on some pleasant Sunday, my father's day at home. Or, when no one else was so inclined, he would take me only. There was a pretty parlor with its simple draperies and furnishings. Nicely bound books on the center table, and its astral lamp and pendants were a fragile affair, but my mother's pride. It was in the living room that we played and really lived. This was separated by glass doors—folding open into the dining room. I will always remember our last company dinner there. Beyond this, a roomy sunny kitchen and a maid.

Grandmother Lathrop was with us that last winter. Also a new baby came December 8, and all was lovely.

Mother had a seamstress, a pretty German girl, who was to come again in the spring to teach me to speak German.

That Christmas season was to be long remembered—and only a memory—not to be repeated for many years. Alas, we had no maid, no pretty parlor, nor lovely living room. I write this for my children—my father's descendants, and in his memory, and not for the public. But that beautiful winter slipped away and spring brought a general commotion, and so regretfully I turn my thoughts away from the lake, the busy river, the cozy comfortable house, and happy carefree days to a new phase of our lives.

## COMMENTARY BY ARTHUR E. HARRINGTON

I am very happy that Lilian remembered so well these early childhood experiences in Milwaukee. Although I mentioned them in my story they were brief and Lilian has given us much more detail and brought to life these very happy family days in Milwaukee.

Lilian has also given me a picture of her father as a warm, loving person. These very likely were some of the happiest days of her life and the life of their whole family. I am sure that Fanny and Grandmother Lathrop enjoyed that love as they shared it caring for them. They would be going to Kansas together, and their family life would be quite different when Edmund's vocation and political life prevented him from being at home. But I am sure that the whole family were proud of him throughout the rest of his life and his many adventures.

Even in his later years in New Mexico when his son Arthur and family lived as neighbors, his grandchildren, including the Arthur Ross family, enjoyed the warm family spirit that his children and his grandchildren enjoyed. I hope that you who are finishing this reading may continue to share the Ross family spirit. May the Lord bless you and keep you!

# B. The First Publication of Edmund G. Ross

## INTRODUCTION BY ARTHUR E. HARRINGTON

Edmund Ross was in his last year in high school at age nine-teen. Continuing with his work with the *Sandusky Mirror*, later known as the *Democratic Mirror*, he was self-supporting. He was also very much aware of what was going on in his country. One of the great issues of the day was capital punishment.

This young man of courage, as we have come to know him, accepted a challenge. The class was assigned a paper to write. He chose to write on this contemporary, controversial issue. This is still an issue for many people. As you read, note that some of the same arguments are used today.

The paper was to be presented, along with other papers of other students, at a meeting at the high school. It proved to be so controversial that the Sandusky High School faculty and adminis-tration became highly disturbed. They threatened to remove him from school if he presented the paper. As we have noted, he chose to leave school.

The editors of the *Mirror*, namely his brother Sylvester Ross and partner William S. Mills, apparently agreed to publish it. One source says that there was so much distortion of what Edmund really said that it should be published to clear the facts.

Among the 104 copies of the *Democratic Mirror* saved by the Follett House Museum, I found this article, which I am sharing with you. I reprint it not for the purpose of convincing you of Ross's opinion concerning capital punishment, but rather that you may come to know some of the thinking of this young man Edmund G. Ross, and that he had the courage to speak about something that was controversial. Secondly, I think you will come to appreciate the high value he placed upon life.

## CAPITAL PUNISHMENT [1845]

As the question of capital punishment is exciting considerable interest in our country, I propose on this occasion, to review some of the arguments which have been advanced in substantiation of its practicability, and also advance some few considerations in favor of its abolition. I know it is argued by some, that this punishment is necessary in order to prevent the commission of crime, and to protect society from the depredations of some lawless characters, who, it is contended can be restrained by no other means—and some have even gone so far as to declare that the abolition of this penalty would be at once, a virtual abolition of all law and government. But if this be the case, if this punishment processes the virtue of preventing crime, as is here alleged, then it follows, necessarily, that the more extensively it is exercised, the better it will be for the community; that it should be inflicted for all crimes as well as that of murder. But that it has not this effect, has been fully demonstrated. In Belgium, Tuscany, Russia, and England, in the old world, and in the state of Vermont, in the new, where it has been either partially or totally abolished, the result has been the actual diminution of crime, as shown by the criminal statistics of those countries.

It may be laid down as an axiom that certainty of punishment is a surer preventive of crime than its severity; and as it is a well-known fact that there is a great and growing reluctance on the part of juries to convict one of murder so long as the penalty is death, it follows, necessarily, that under this code the punishment of crime is at least uncertain.

The frequent accounts which we have of the execution of innocent men, charged with murder, and convicted and sentenced upon false testimony, is of itself, I think, sufficient evidence that the repeal of this iniquitous institution should be demanded by every benevolent feeling of the human heart. But it is said, in answer to this, the innocent may still suffer, if imprisonment should be substituted. Although this would undoubtedly be the case, to some extent, one thing is here forgotten; that is, that the accused person is deprived of nothing but his liberty, which can be easily restored when proved innocent.

Another argument in favor of its repeal, and one which should have great weight with every mind that reveres the doctrines of pure and undefiled religion, is that it teaches, by example, the most faithful of all modes of teaching, the wicked principle of revenge: of taking an eye for an eye, and a tooth for a tooth in opposition to the teaching of him who bade his disciples that they "resist not evil—but whosoever shall smite thee on thy right cheek, turn to him the other also." It seeks to repair an injury done to society, by committing another of the same stamp; and it is calculated to lessen, in the minds of its upholders, the sacredness of human life.

It is probably admitted by all, that the paramount objects of legal punishment should be the reformation of the offender, and the protection of society. And how are these to be accomplished? Is it by condemning the criminal as an enemy to his race and unworthy of the enjoyment of society of men, and even life, and for that reason casting him out of the world? Certainly not. For that would be but aggravating the evil; as it would be placing the offender beyond all further influences, both good and evil, so far as this world is concerned and that it fails in the second mentioned object, is proved by the decrease of crime in those countries in which the death penalty has been abolished. And not only this, but it deprives society of the benefits, which it cannot be denied would, in many cases, result from the exercise of mercy and forbearance towards the criminal.

But there is another consideration, which, with me, had more weight than anything else. I contend that man has no right to deprive a fellow being of that life which he gave not, and which he cannot restore, or to inflict upon him any pain whatever, as punishment merely; and for this reason, that he is incapable of exercising that strict and equal justice which the punishment of crime requires. If the rights of society are invaded, what more can be reasonable than to be defended from further depredations of the offending member, by placing him in such a situation, and under such influences, as are calculated to secure his reformation and restoration to virtue? I ask which best comports with the dictates of reason and benevolence? Which most strongly commends itself to the sympathies of the human heart—this method, or the rigorous and cruel one now pursued? But it is argued in opposition, that this penalty must be executed, or our Maker disobeyed. The language of the Apostle is quoted—"The powers that be are ordained of God." Hence, it is argued, we must be obedient unto those powers, or incur the Divine displeasure. But it is only necessary to observe, in answer to this, that the same argument might have been urged with equal propriety, and with equal force, in favor of the continuance of the Mosaic dispensation, or the Roman Church in its balmiest days, or any other state of things which has ever existed. But says one, would you inflict no punishment?—would you inflict no punishment?—would you allow the vile murderer to go "unwhipt of justice?" In the infliction of pain for the purpose of causing suffering on the part of the criminal, is here meant by punishment? I answer, I would; for what is the effect of such course, but to aggravate the evil? As it is well-known by everyone who has any knowledge of human nature, that it is calculated rather to confirm the transgressor in his ways than otherwise.

And again, I would ask if those penalties attached to the physical and moral laws which the Governor of the Universe has established, are not enough so far as the abstract matter of punishment is concerned.

I am aware that this is an unpopular sentiment—that theologians and statesmen have combined in denouncing it—but I ask, is it not in accordance with the express declarations of sacred writ, that "God is a God that judgeth in the earth," that he and the righteous are recompensed in the earth, much more than the wicked and the sinner"; and also in accordance with the well-known fact that pain, physical and mental, is the necessary result of disobedience to the laws which govern our existence.

It is proposed, by many of the opposers of this institution, that solitary confinement for life be substituted; but this, it appears to me, would be little if any, improvement; as the result would be nearly the same as the immediate infliction of death.

The criminal, although he might become a reformed man, could still be of no further use either to himself or to the world, and thus life itself would be rendered a curse to him; and by an experiment made in the state prison of New York in the year 1821, in the solitary confinement of 80 criminals, it is proved that this mode of punishment has a strong tendency to produce insanity, and is also destructive of life, so that the crime of murder would still rest upon society, as much in one case as the other, as it matters not whether you kill a man suddenly, or by inches; it is alike murder in both cases.

But what appears to me to be truly astonishing is that the advocates of this institution have attempted to sustain it by arguments drawn from the sacred Scriptures. The words "Whoso sheddeth man's blood, by man shall his blood be shed," are quoted. Now by the same mode of reasoning, it may be proved equally conclusive that it is a violation of God's law to take the life or eat the flesh of any animal, as it is written, in immediate connection with the verse already quoted. "But flesh with the life thereof, which is the blood thereof, shall not eat." Now, in order to be consistent, those who attempt to sustain capital punishment by Scripture arguments, must, it appears to me, refrain from the use of animal food. But this they do not do: esteeming their appetites, it would seem, paramount in authority to the Bible command.

But it is argued, on the other hand, that this command, "Whoso sheddeth man's blood," etc., was in force before the Jews had a national existence, and was not, therefore, peculiar to that dispensation, but merely incorporated into it. But this does not alter the case; for it cannot be denied that it did constitute a part of the Mosaic law, and as it was not recognized by Christ at the introduction of the new, or Christian dispensation, it cannot be made obligatory upon us.

It is contended, again, that, as man was created in the image of his Maker, the murder of him, by his fellow man, is the most heinous of all crimes and demands, consequently, the severest penalty which can be inflicted. But the same argument, if it has any weight, might be urged with equal propriety and with equal force in favor of the execution of every hangman in the land.

It may not perhaps be generally known, that in some parts of our country, this punishment is more extensively exercised than in others. In the state of South Carolina, for instance, the crime of theft, however paltry the sum purloined, is punishable with death. In the District of Columbia, also, the crime of arson, unless a reformation has been effected within four or five years, when committed by a person whom God, in his wisdom, has seen proper to clothe with a sable skin, and whom man, in his wickedness, has deprived of his natural rights, and compelled to ignominious servitude, is punished by the beheading of the offender. And as if this were not enough, as if the lifeless form could still be made to feel the effects of that savage, brutal, and disgusting spirit which delights in the misery of its victims, he is quartered and placed in the most public parts of the district. This too, in a territory under the immediate supervision of what has been frequently and boastingly termed the most free and enlightened government on earth. But this is not to be wondered. It is but one of the legitimate effects of that spirit which prompts the legal murder of our erring brethren; and may the time soon come, when this relic of barbarity shall cease to disgrace our statutes.

## COMMENTARY BY ARTHUR E. HARRINGTON

As I have been typing the above I have been impressed with Edmund's extensive vocabulary. He has had only three years of high school, and he was only nineteen years of age.

Edmund was also very well read on his subject as to what had been going on in many parts of the world and in his own country. He also was writing with deep commitment. He expressed a very high value on human life, even the lives of those who desecrate life. He also, at this early age, had an awareness of and faith in the Creator of the universe, the earth, and sacredness of life. This foundation undergirded all that he did throughout his career as a publisher, a soldier responsible for his men, as a senator voting on critical issues, as a governor responsible for a growing territory, and most of all as a husband and a father. I hope you have enjoyed and been inspired by his early writing.

# C. Edmund G. Ross Chronology
## by Paul H. Carlson

December 7, 1826—Born, Ashland, Ohio, son of Sylvester Flint Ross and Cynthia Rice (3rd of 14 children). (EB, 15)

1837—Apprenticed to Henry C. Grey, owner and editor of the [*Huron Commercial Advertiser*]. (EB, 16)

1841—Brother Sylvester purchases printing plant in Sandusky, Ohio. Starts *Sandusky Mirror*. Edmund accompanies to work in *Mirror* office. (EB, 16)

Spring, 1847—Journeys to Janesville, Wisconsin, to spend summer on farm purchased by father. December returns to Sandusky, Ohio. (EB)

1848—Casts first vote (for Van Buren and Charles Francis Adams). (EB, 18)

October 15, 1848—Marries Fannie [sp] Maria Lathrop, born New York State, daughter of Rodney Lathrop. (KHS document)

1849—Asiatic cholera kills several Ross and Lathrop family members. (EB, 18)

1850—Daughter born. (EB, 19)

1852—Edmund, Fannie [sp] and baby daughter move to Wisconsin. Settle in Milwaukee. Edmund and brother work for *Milwaukee Free Democrat*. (EB, 19)

1854—Edmund and William Ross participate in freeing fugitive slave. S. M. Booth, their boss, is participant causing publication of *Free Democrat* to be suspended. Brothers secure better positions with *Milwaukee Daily Sentinel*. (EB, 19–20)

1856—Trained as printer, Ross is foreman at *Milwaukee Daily Sentinel*. Three children, daughter, 6; son, 3; baby born December 1855. Volunteers to emigrate to Kansas where conflict over slavery. Publishes the *Tribune*. (KHS document)

May 20, 1856—Edmund heads party out of Milwaukee to Kansas "to fight for freedom." (EB, 25) At Janesville, Wisconsin, joined by remainder of Ross family.

August 11, 1856—Ross family welcomed to Topeka, Kansas. (EB, 30)

December, 1856—Edmund Ross buys interest of John Speer in *Kansas Tribune* in Topeka making him partners with brother William. Paper run by brothers. (EB, 38)

August 26, 1857—Grasshopper Falls Convention, Kansas. Free state men decide to participate in territorial election set for October instead of ignoring the territorial government by refusing to vote. Edmund was the secretary of the convention. (EB, 39)

October 18, 1858—Edmund retires from *Tribune* and moves to Wabaunsee County. (EB, 39)

Summer, 1859—As delegate to Wyandotte Constitutional Convention has prominent part in shaping Kansas constitution. (EB)

October, 1859—Edmund and William Ross establish new paper in Topeka, *The Kansas State Record*. Edmund's influential writing will include promoting the railroad convention of 1860. (EB, 39)

September, 1860—Ross identified with attempt of Col. Cyrus K. Holliday to organize the Atlantic & Santa Fe Railroad. (Ross later turned the first spadeful of earth in ceremony starting construction of AT&SF)

August, 1862—*State Record* is sold to S. D. MacDonald and F. G. Adams. Edmund begins recruiting a company which becomes Company E of the Eleventh Kansas Regiment. Ross is elected captain and company goes to Leavenworth to join regiment commanded by Col. Samuel J. (EB, 47)

1863—Regiment returns to Kansas City, reorganized as cavalry regiment and Ross appointed major by Governor Carney. Duties include protecting Lawrence, Kansas, where massacre occurred. Guard town for eight months. (EB, 47)

September, 1864—Part of Eleventh Kansas participates in the Battle of the Little Blue, a few miles east of Kansas City. The Confederate army had been heading toward Fort Leavenworth, Kansas, when confronted by Union forces. Maj. Edmund Ross has two horses shot from under him during a day of severe fighting. (EB, 50)

Sept. 20, 1865—Edmund mustered out of military service. (EB, 55)

July 20, 1866—Appointed U.S. Senator from Kansas replacing Lane whose actions in Senate angered Kansans. (EB, 56)

January, 1868—Ross elected by Kansas legislature to the U.S. Senate (KHS document)

May 16, 1868—Votes "not guilty" on President Andrew Johnson's impeachment.

March 3, 1871—Concludes term as U.S. senator and returns to Kansas.

May 18, 1871—Rosses deed ground to City of Lawrence, Kansas, "Beginning at a point 250 feet west of the Southwest corner of Tennessee Street and Adams Street then south 195 feet, west 80 feet, north 195 feet, east 80 feet to beginning, being that part of Ohio Street south of Adams Street in the City of Lawrence."

Late 1871—Starts paper at Coffeyville, Kansas.

April 23, 1872—Tornado destroys Coffeyville newspaper plant. Ross returns to Lawrence; is associated with newspaper work including publisher of *The Standard*.

February, 1880—Buys *Leavenworth Press*, moves *Standard* there and consolidates two papers.

Fall, 1880—"Decisive defeat" as a candidate for governorship of Kansas in opposing incumbent St. John.

1882—Arrives in Albuquerque to work at printers case at *Albuquerque Journal*. (SMS biography)

1883—Editor of the *Albuquerque Democrat*.

July, 1884—Establishes residence in Albuquerque.

June 15, 1885—Assumes governorship of New Mexico.

May, 1886—Ross reorganizes Bureau of Immigration personally taking charge of getting it off the ground. (Shane)

July, 1886—Removes territorial treasurer Antonio Ortiz y Salazar from office. (Shane, 56)

1888—Inaugurates college in Las Cruces. This act creates University of New Mexico and School of Mines. (Shane, 87)

1889—Signs enabling act for three New Mexico colleges.

April 17, 1889—Ross replaced by Bradford Prince as Governor.

1890—Becomes editor of *Deming Headlight*.

1893—Article, "A Reminiscence of the Kansas Conflict," published in Albuquerque by Ross.

1894—Secretary of Territorial Bureau of Immigration for two years.

1896—Practiced law in Albuquerque and lived on ranch three-and-one-half miles south of town on Broadway. This was the "soldier's claim" land. (Lillian [sp] Ross Lies [sp] Paper #3, KHS document)

1896—*History of the Impeachment of Andrew Johnson, President of the United States, by the House of Representatives, and His Trial by the Senate for High Crimes and Misdemeanors in Office, 1868*, published in Santa Fe.

1898—Ross and Fannie [sp] celebrate fiftieth anniversary. (EB)

Nov. 12, 1899—Fannie [sp] Ross dies.

1901—Lived at 920 Barelas Road, a "retired journalist."

1905—Moves to 1216 W. Railroad (Central) Ave. with Pitt. (Lillian [sp] Ross Leis)

March 3, 1907—Gen. Hugh Cameron, the "Kansas Hermit," arrives with letters of commendation and apology from Kansas. (KHS document)

May 8, 1907—11:00 a.m., Ross dies in Albuquerque, New Mexico, after three-days' bout with pneumonia at eighty years, five months, one day. (Fairview Cemetery in Albuqeruque, New Mexico document)

May 10, 1907—Ross's funeral. (French Mortuary—NMG Sept. 1874, p. 72)

# D. Newspaper Articles

## Edmund G. Ross Dies at Age of Four Score

### Man Who Saved President Johnson From Impeachment Closes Eventful Career in This City

#### Kansas Senator and New Mexico Governor

### Death Follows Closely on Honorable Vindication at Hands of People of Kansas and of the Country

Edmund G. Ross United States senator from Kansas in 1867-71, and governor of New Mexico under the administration of President Cleveland, died at his home in this city at 11 o'clock yesterday morning after three days' illness with pneumonia. Mr. Ross was eighty-one years of age and his death closes one of the most eventful and noted careers in the history of the country. It was Senator Ross who, in 1868, following his convictions in the face of certain political ruin, cast the deciding vote which saved President Andrew Johnson from impeachment for high crimes and misdemeanors. The impeachment, it is now widely recognized, would have been a national disgrace. Ross was practically exiled from Kansas as a result of his action, and for a quarter of a century was the object of the bitterest hatred on the part of the people of that state. Only a few months ago did his belated vindication come after Senator Ross had spent many years in retirement patiently awaiting for his maligners to admit they had wronged him. The vindication was formally expressed to Senator Ross when General Hugh Cameron, the "Kansas Hermit" made his remarkable pilgrimage to this city from his hut on the banks of the Kaw to hear messages of appreciation from the people of the Sunflower state to Senator Ross. General Cameron, a life-long friend and war comrade of Senator Ross, brought with him letters from Governor Hatch of Kansas, from the lieutenant governor, and both houses of the legislature, prominent editors and statesmen, acknowledging the wrong that was done Senator Ross and expressing appreciation of the high motives which prompted his vote in the impeachment trial.

Mr. Ross is survived by five children—Pitt Ross, of this city, county surveyor; Mrs. W. H. Cobb, wife of the Gold Avenue photographer; Mrs. George Leis, of Lawrence Kans., whose husband is depot advertising agent for the Santa Fe; Kay Ross, of Bisbee, Ariz.; Mrs. George H. Miles of San Paula, Cal. The deceased is also survived by three sisters and two brothers as follows: Mrs. Judge Bennett of Silver City, Mrs. N. A. Wemple, of Kansas City, Kans., Charles Ross of Santa Ana, Cal. and Walter Ross of Detroit, Mich., and Mrs. E. M. Hewens of Oklahoma.

The arrangements for the funeral were not perfected yesterday, but it is understood the services will be held at the Presbyterian church on Friday afternoon. Further details will be announced later. Senator Ross, at one time a figure of national prominence has been one of the foremost and most distinguished citizens of New Mexico for many years, and his funeral will likely be one of the largest ever held in this city.

—*Albuquerque Morning Journal*, May 9, 1907

## SENATOR ROSS' CAREER

Edmund G. Ross was born in Ashland, Huron County, Ohio December 7, 1826. At ten he entered a printing office. In 1847 he traveled through Indiana, Illinois and Wisconsin as a journeyman printer, and was married in 1848 to Miss Fannie [sp] M. Lathrop, a native of New York. Seven children were born of the marriage, Mrs. Ross dying in 1899 after fifty-one years of wedded life. As a newspaper man, Ross was employed on the [*Milwaukee Free Democrat*], the [*Milwaukee Sentinel*], the Lawrence, [*Kansas Tribune*] and the [*Topeka Tribune*], which he founded, in 1859, after serving with the "Free State Troops" in the border wars he was elected a member of the Wyandotte constitutional convention, which framed the constitution under which the territory of Kansas was admitted into the union. He founded the Kansas State Record, since become the Topeka Capitol, in partnership with his brother, and the two erected the first three-story concrete building exclusively for newspaper purposes in Kansas.

In 1862 Ross raised a company of volunteers in Topeka for the support of the union cause, became its captain and, in 1864 was promoted to major of the Eleventh Kansas Infantry. He served as colonel of battalion during the Price raid, and participated in many engagements at one time having [three horses shot] under him and his shoulder straps shot away. He served all through the war, principally along the Kansas-Missouri border. After the war, Ross published the [*Kansas Tribune*] at Lawrence . . . Kansas in 1866 appointed Ross to the seat in the senate made vacant by the suicide of James Lane and in 1867 he was elected by the legislature to the office for the term of 1867-71.

On his return to Kansas after the impeachment trial Ross was refused work on various newspapers through the work of the political ring which feared to see him get back into politics. He went to Coffeyville, Kan. and for several years published "Ross' Paper" exposing political corruption in the state, his plant being finally destroyed by a cyclone. Returning to Lawrence in 1873, he founded the "Evening Paper" and as its editor procured the downfall of United States Senator Pomeroy. Later he and his son published the "Spirit of Kansas", a weekly, at Lawrence . . . afterward becoming foreman of the Lawrence Journal. Later, he helped issue the "Daily Standard" at Lawrence. In 1880 he came to New Mexico and went to work at the printer's case on the Albuquerque Journal, remaining there until his appointment as governor by Cleveland in 1885.

—*Albuquerque Morning Journal*, May 9, 1907

## WAGED WAR ON GRAFTERS

Governor Ross had probably the most tempestuous administration in the history of the territory as one of the most corrupt rings ever in power ruled New Mexico, and his fight against it was determined, bitter, at times unavailing and always strenuous. The legislature ran wild and passed some of the most iniquitous laws on record over his veto. After leaving office Ross entered the office of the New Mexican at Santa Fe as a typesetter, going from there to Deming where he edited the [Deming Headlight]. During the first two years of the administration of Governor Thornton, Ross was secretary of the bureau of immigration. Since 1895 he had lived in retirement in this city, after one of the most varied and remarkable careers in the country's annals.

On of the most historical works of the period is the book on the impeachment of Johnson written and published by Mr. Ross, an introduction which is written by David H. Hill. The work is a stirring recital of the events leading up to and following the great crisis, the impeachment trial, and fully sets forth Mr. Ross' motives in voting against impeachment.

—*Albuquerque Morning Journal*, May 9, 1907

## THE LATE EDMUND G. ROSS

The death of Hon. Edmund G. Ross, ex-governor of New Mexico, which occurred at the family residence in this city at noon Wednesday, marked the severing of one of the few links that had remained between the present age of peace and good will and the age of blood and iron—the days that tried men's souls, in the United States. His life led through the whole of the stormiest period in the nation's history, and he personally took an active part in many of the stormiest features of that era of upheaval and revolution.

A citizen of Kansas in the days of John Brown, of Ossawattamie, he took a conspicuous part in the proceedings of that time which attracted the attention of the world, and which were the opening skirmishes of the battle which was soon to follow—the great struggle between liberty and slavery, for the supremacy on the American continent. At the first call to arms in defense of the old flag he recruited a company for the First Kansas regiment, entered as its captain, was promoted to be major of the Eleventh regiment, and was later appointed by the governor of the state to fill a vacancy in the United States senate—an appointment that was afterward ratified through an election by the legislature. From this it will be seen that his service as a soldier was clearly of such a character as to commend him favorably to his superior officers in the army, and his fellow citizens of the state. As a senator in congress his record was without a blemish, and he was endorsed and upheld by the people of his state in everything he did, up to the time that he cast his vote against the conviction of President Johnson. He knew at the time he cast that vote of "not guilty" would cost him the sympathy and support of his state, because Kansas at that time was perfectly frantic for the removal of Johnson, and would not listen to reason from any source, but he realized that while his own political existence was in the balance on the one side, the existence of the free institutions of the United States hung on the other, and his vote being sufficient to turn the scale, he chose to sacrifice himself to preserve the life of the government and for a great many years of his no martyr to the cause of right and justice ever suffered more hostility, more contumely, more ostracism, more cruel persecution at the hands of his fellow men, than Edmund G. Ross suffered for an act that saved his country from inevitable anarchy—for it is admitted by all that had the impeachment of Johnson been successful it would have established a precedent leading to the removal of the president whenever there might happen to be a hot headed opposition in congress, and our attitude before the world would probably have been by this time about the same as that of the little warring republics of South America.

But there is great reason for gratification in the fact that he lived long enough to know that time had vindicated his course, and that while the world could never undo the wrong it had done him, it had at least acknowledged its error, and accorded him the merit he deserved for his patriotism, his courage, and his self-sacrifice in the cause of his country and humanity. Though his vindication came late it was not too late to show him that in his

case, at least, truth was not to be forever on the scaffold with
error ever on the throne. His sun went down in a cloudless sky,
and no one who believes in the justice of God or the efficacy of
the sacrifice on Calvary can doubt for a moment that [he] found
laid up for him a crown [of] righteousness.
                          —*Albuquerque Morning Journal*, May 10, 1907


## EDMUND G. ROSS DEATH

After retirement as governor, Edmund G. Ross went to work in
printer's trade and in 1899 assumed the editorial management of
the [*Deming Headlight*]. Remained in charge of the Headlight
until 1893 and during this time, wrote a history of the impeachment trial which is a valuable literary and historical production.
Later on he served as Secretary of the Bureau of Immigration at
Santa Fe. In recent years, he has resided quietly at Albuquerque.

He lived to see his course in all his public life vindicated both by
press and public. He died after having rounded out a career
full of honor, respected by all who knew him.
                          —*Deming Headlight*, May 16, 1907